A bold and courageous endeavor ... our modern day, this compilation of essays is written primarily by women for women. Yet this is not a book about women but about God. The diverse voices representing various lived experiences of sisters across the US will serve this changing generation of Christians well. Authors uncompromisingly approach the manifold social and familial issues in contemporary society with Scriptural fidelity. They offer practical solutions and brilliantly address everyday challenges of life with honesty and sincerity. *Beyond the Roles* provides us with the gift of viewing our long-held values with a renewed spiritual perspective.

ALEXANDER JUN, PhD
Professor of Higher Education, Azusa Pacific University

With growing biblical illiteracy and a culture oriented toward self, *Beyond the Roles* is a book I urge every Christian woman to read. It is Theology 101 and Practical Theology packaged together to highlight the necessity of the gospel as both our "fighting words," and the lens in which we view all of life. It is a book I imagine will not leave our relationships, churches and communities unchanged.

KRISTEN HATTON
Author of *The Gospel-Centered Life in Exodus for Students, Face Time: Your Identity in a Selfie World,* and *Get Your Story Straight.*

In a world where everything seems fluid, we need clear and kind gospel truth. Deeply theologically grounded, *Beyond the Roles* draws from a rich diversity of female voices to explore how women living out the gospel isn't a function of roles, but rather part of the *imago dei.* As such, it gives hope for weary women and for the flourishing of the entire church.

ASHLEY HALES
Author of *Finding Holy in the Suburbs*

Beyond the Roles is an excellent collection of essays offering a biblical perspective on various issues relevant to the task of women's discipleship. Each topic receives intellectually rigorous yet accessible treatment and is delivered with an encouraging tone. As a whole, the book reinforces the fact that the church needs women and their God-given gifts in order to thrive as Christ's bride, and the authors do a great service to all who participate in or influence contemporary women's ministry.

MELISSA CAIN TRAVIS, PhD
Assistant Professor, Houston Baptist University

In this wonderful volume, a varied and gifted collection of authors offer invaluable, biblically-grounded perspective on a host of issues related to women's ministry. *Beyond the Roles'* contributors demonstrate an admirable commitment to and facility with the Scriptures, taking care to ground their approach to their chosen subject in the timeless truths of God's Word. In an age when the church cannot afford to lose its moorings in biblical truth, this collection provides an excellent guide to both women and men who want to see the body of Christ equipped for faithful and effective women's ministry.

J. DEREK HALVORSON, PhD
President, Covenant College

Beyond the Roles is an eminently readable and bracingly practical guide to women's ministry that breaks out of the usual mold to address the most pressing issues of the day and integrate women into the church from every circumstance and life situation. No matter the size, no matter the resources, whether your church has a formal women's ministry or not, the voices in this book will set you on a solid course not only for reaching out and equipping women for the service of the kingdom but also for empowering them to engage the world for Christ.

ANNE KENNEDY
Blogger at patheos.com/blogs/preventinggrace, and author of
Nailed It: 365 Sarcastic Devotions for Angry and Worn-Out People

I can't think of anyone more qualified to shepherd a book on women's ministry than the general editor Melanie Cogdill. Thus *Beyond the Roles* is biblically faithful, theologically rich, and also amazingly practical. For example, it offers wisdom on everything from racial healing to gender dysphoria, domestic abuse, to helping cope with fears (even FoMO—the fear of missing out). *Beyond the Roles* is refreshing and desperately needed in this world that questions even the definition of what it means to be male or female.

CLAY JONES
Associate Professor of Christian Apologetics, Talbot School of Theology.
Author of *Why Does God Allow Evil?: Compelling Answers to Life's Toughest Questions* and of *Immortal: How the Fear of Death Drives Us and What We Can Do About It* (April 2020).

This team effort weds insightful counsel on a variety of discipleship topics with thoughtfully addressed biblical foundations. The book also models its intent, namely a positive articulation of Christian women bearing witness at work, in community life, within the Church, and through redemptive relationships. I especially appreciate how each chapter includes reflection questions for personal and group use. As general editor Melanie Cogdill points out, there are far too few books like this one. I hope this solid installment leads to many more.

DONALD C. GUTHRIE, EdD
Professor of Educational Ministries, Trinity Evangelical Divinity School

Foreword by Irwyn Ince

BEYOND THE ROLES

A Biblical Foundation for Women and Ministry

GENERAL EDITOR MELANIE COGDILL

DISCIPLESHIP MINISTRIES

© 2019 – Melanie Cogdill

Published by:
Committee on Discipleship Ministries
1700 North Brown Road, Suite 102
Lawrenceville, Georgia 30043
Bookstore: 1-800-283-1357
678-825-1100
www.pcacdm.org/bookstore

Cover and interior design: Dwayne Cogdill, www.saintdwayne.com

Database(C) 2001 iExalt, Inc.

ISBN: 978-1-944964-43-6

For Susan Hunt
and all her spiritual daughters
and granddaughters
(Psalm 78:5-7).

Contents

Foreword
Rev. Dr. Irwyn Ince

From 2016-17, I had the privilege of serving as the chair of the Presbyterian Church in America's (PCA) study committee on the role of women in the ministry of the church. Our committee was comprised of a group of men and women who joyfully embrace our denomination's biblical and confessional commitments. Simultaneously, within that embrace, we brought to the table a diversity of perspectives on the issue.

For some, the PCA studying the issue of women in the ministry of the church in 2016 was offensive. There was nothing to study. Our culture has progressed beyond the point of asserting that there should be any distinction between the ways women and men should serve in ministry. They thought that taking up the issue reflected backward, misogynistic views that ought to be left to die in the past.

There were others who offered a similar critique—there was nothing to study—but for a different reason. The Bible is clear on the roles of men and women in the church. It was a settled matter, and our denomination was doing well in following biblical principles. Some thought to take up the issue as a denomination indicated we are drifting away from orthodox Christian beliefs and into theological liberalism. We were on the dreaded "slippery slope."

Between these two camps we found ourselves holding to biblical authority for the life of faith. This meant not only affirming gender distinctions, but it also meant an active pursuit of ensuring room and opportunity for women to flourish and exercise their God-given gifts to be used to further His kingdom and used for the good of His church. Whenever and wherever this is not happening, it wounds the body of Christ. Your local church is not as beautiful or effective as she is called to be without the gifts of women in the church. As we stated in our report, "Male and female interdependence is a key element of the local church, for 'in the Lord woman is not independent of man nor man of woman; for as woman was made from man, so now man is born of woman. And all things are from God'" (1 Cor. 11:11-12).

The Holy Spirit gives gifts to men and women in the body of Christ for the common good, and He does not discriminate (1 Cor. 12:4-11). While the Lord is not silent about roles, spiritual gifts are not gender specific. The Holy Spirit doesn't limit the gift of teaching only to men, nor does He limit the gift of care only to women. This truth is on full display in the pages that follow. Listen to and learn from these women!

I'm well aware that *Beyond the Roles: A Biblical Foundation for Women and Ministry* targets a primarily female audience who serve in women's ministries in their church. Yet, the opportunity to write this foreword is a gift to me. I know some of these authors personally and have gleaned from their wisdom over the years. I've quoted at least two of these contributors in my past sermons. Some of these writers I only know online. But now I'm blessed to have learned from all of the authors who contributed to this book.

I don't know of another book on women's ministry that has a richer tapestry of voices. They come from a lavish diversity of ethnic, cultural, and generational backgrounds. Reader, you will benefit from this. Just as one ethnic group and cultural perspective on our faith dominates the majority of churches in America, so it is with most books on any ministry issue—the view of one author. What you have in your hands is different. And it is beautiful. With their diverse voices these women tackle topics that are timely for our age with wisdom they have gleaned from the timeless Word of God. Can the church be a city of refuge in the #MeToo and #ChurchToo age? How do Christian women pursue authentic friendships across lines of difference? What are the implications of the *Imago Dei* for women in ministry? What does the pursuit of racial healing in women's ministry look like? Wisdom. Leadership. Discipleship. Singleness. The gospel. The kingdom. Take up and read!

Thank you, sisters, for this work. It is a gift to God's church—men and women, young and old.

Rev. Dr. Irwyn Ince serves as a pastor at Grace DC Presbyterian Church (www.gracedc.net) and is the director of the Grace DC Institute for Cross-Cultural Mission (www.gracedc.institute).

Preface

Melanie Cogdill

Professionally, I am the managing editor of a theological magazine, and as such, I receive hundreds of review copies of books each year. I have tall stacks of books covering my desk. Many of them, frankly, cover issues that have been written by others before. As I look through books every week, I ask myself, why did the author write this? What does this book contribute to the issue that it addresses? Is this book worth an investment of my time to read? There are so many books out there, why does it matter that this one exists?

Not only do I receive review copies of books for work (many of which I did not request), I also am on the hunt for books as resources to equip Christians to grow in their faith by understanding theological truths. With this purpose in mind, a couple of years ago at the Evangelical Theology Society convention I attended for work, I walked the exhibitors hall to see what books were available from the many publishers displaying highlights of their catalog. Since I am involved in women's ministry in my local church and in my denomination, I started noticing there were very few books addressed to women as the primary audience. The ones on display for women in particular focused on the roles women have in seasons of their lives, particularly on parenting and marriage. Granted, this theological conference does not focus on women's ministry or women in ministry, but it made me take note that many non-academic Christian books marketed to women address *only* parenting or marriage.

In the past ten years you can count on one hand books (and, by that, I mean one book) like this one that are a compilation of issues written by a collective of various authors on the topic of women's ministry. This is not a prescriptive how-to book that gives you a "top 10 tips" list for a "successful" women's ministry.

The intent of this book is to address a few contemporary issues women's ministry leadership faces as they minister to women in their churches. For example, five years ago women's ministry didn't have to grapple with ministering to transgendered-identifying people. But Western mores have shifted, and now gender-identity issues are at the forefront of cultural conversations. What does Scripture say about gender identity?

In addition, in the United States, the evangelical church has historically been ethnically homogenous. What does it mean for leaders in women's ministry to reflect the biblical truth of the people of God being made up of every tribe and tongue and people?

One of the most encouraging parts of this project has been connecting with the various women who author these chapters. A couple of writers are long-time ministry partners and friends, some are acquaintances, and others are new contacts altogether. It is amazing to see such diversity represented in these pages, not only ethnically with African-American and Asian writers, but also across generations from 20-something Millennials to Baby Boomers. While there is diversity among the authors in this book, there are also many commonalities among these women—all of them are thoughtful, intelligent, and most of all, they love Christ and serve His Church.

The purpose of this book is two-fold, which is why the book is divided into two parts. One is to posit that women's ministry that lasts instead of fizzles needs to be built on a theological foundation (the content of part one) and not on the latest hip event or ministry trend. The issues and challenges we face in ministry might morph and change over the years, but the foundation on which we address those issues must be rooted in Scripture. Second, it's to bring thoughtful essays to readers to consider issues that face women's ministry or that ministry to women should grapple with during this particular time in the 21st century (the content of part two).

As a Women's Ministry Trainer for the Presbyterian Church in America (PCA) I hold to and teach complementarianism. I do not advocate for or believe in the ordination of women as either teaching or ruling elders (and neither do any of these contributors). However, you will not find any chapters dealing with the role of women in the church. There are many academic books and essays that deal with that issue in-depth. This book is also written by women who are members of and attend churches in my denomination (Presbyterian Church in America—PCA), but our readership, we pray, is not limited to women in the PCA; it is for readers who serve as women's ministry leaders, and for readers who know and interact with Christian women. These truths are relevant to all Christian women and transcend denominational lines.

My prayer is that this content will not only help you contextualize your ministry, but also challenge you to build a women's ministry on theological truth so that each woman who attends your church is encouraged in her faith and equipped to live a life that reflects the glory of God.

Melanie Cogdill is a women's ministry trainer for the Presbyterian Church in America, the managing editor of the CHRISTIAN RESEARCH JOURNAL (equip.org), and host of the weekly podcast *Postmodern Realities* (available on iTunes).

Introduction

Live for the Line, Not the Dot
Karen Hodge

A dot is a single fixed point. A woman's life is filled with innumerable dots. She sets goals and makes her plans. Dots are things we treasure, value, and prioritize. They are the things in which we invest our lives. Dots can be things such as an education, job, marriage, financial security, or having children. These things are good gifts from God, but they should never become ultimate things in a woman's life. I believe a woman is a product of her doxology. What she worships is reflected in her life. The word "worship" finds its roots in the words "shape" and "worthy." What she worships, values, or elevates as worthy profoundly shapes everything about her; it ultimately sets the trajectory for her life.

A line is a continuous segment between two fixed points. For the believer, the line is infinite and eternal. It begins in eternity past when, ". . . he chose us in him before the foundation of the world, that we should be holy and blameless before him" (Eph. 1:4). It ends in eternity future. As He says, "I am the Alpha and the Omega, the first and the last, the beginning and the end" (Rev. 22:13). Our temporal and earthly line is lived between birth and death. We walk it day in and day out "by faith, not by sight" (2 Cor. 5:7). What a woman is looking to, the things which captivate her attention, and the forces driving her may be the greatest indicators of whether she is living for the line or the dot. The dot is temporal, and the line is eternal. Paul says, ". . . we look not to the things that are seen but to the things that are unseen. For the things that are seen are transient, but the things that are unseen are eternal" (2 Cor. 4:18). Whether you are living for the dot (temporal) or living for the line (eternal) has everything to do with where you fix your eyes. We become what we behold. The greatest part of a woman's life is unseen.

The timeline over the last century has highlighted countless dots for women. These dots are constantly fluctuating. We have more access to education, new vocational fields are open to us, and we have acquired the right to vote. Every decade has brought about new cultural norms about what it means for men and women to relate to one another. What women traditionally do, where we can go, and how we communicate have all changed. It would be nearly impossible to track all the hair and clothing styles that have evolved. Society has sought to alter how we define gender to the point where they want to erase the idea of womanhood altogether. Even with all these changes, some things never change. These are the things located along the line. These truths are eternal, and they transcend culture, time, and generations.

God's design for womanhood is not a dot; it is an enduring line. He spoke creation into existence establishing His Word as our authority (Gen. 1:1). The man's and woman's gender distinctiveness as image-bearers is a necessary dimension to reflect who God is (Gen. 1:27). Eve's companionship with Adam answered his "not good" isolation. Her helper design is a suitable fit complementing every relationship and calling (Gen. 2:18). She was created to be equal in being but diverse in function in every context of life (Gen. 1:27). Their oneness together reflects the community existing in the Godhead (Gen. 2:24). They were put on a mission to spread Eden to the ends of the earth (Gen. 1:28). Their designs were intended to reflect His glory, not their own. Their choice to seek to be Godlike and move towards independence brought about the brokenness of everything and every person (Gen. 3). These biblical truths about our design never change.

Believing these things is counter-cultural. As this century progresses, the indicators are it will only become harder, not easier, to embrace these truths. Women will be forced to choose. Will we cave to the culture (conformation) or will we yield to the potential of a greater change for the glory of God (transformation)? Transformation is radical and often complicated. It is rarely convenient and seldom comfortable, but at the end of the line, it is ultimately glorious. Women need to be transformed by the "renewing of their mind" (Rom. 12:1-2). Our "dot-like" thinking and living need to be renovated.

This is a strategic moment in time when we must be steadfast in helping women to think and live biblically and live in the context of the church community. Word-based and relationally-driven women's ministry encourages women to understand who God is and who He created us to be. It is intended to equip women to fulfill our creation design in whatever context we are called—the home, church, workplace, or community. It should be gospel-centered in both its teaching and application. Womanhood will either be defined biblically, or it will be defined culturally.

We need women leaders to be in-the-world-but-not-of-the-world. A leader has been defined as someone who goes before or comes alongside others to bring them to a desired destination. We have much to glean from leaders who have gone before us and shown us the shape of godliness. More often than not we are influenced by godly older women (spiritual mothers) and gospel friends who are fellow pilgrims, coming alongside us as we live along the line. For women of faith, the omega-fixed point, the desired destination at the end of the line, is Heaven.

Why do you do what you do? How you answer this question reveals whether you are living for the line or the dot. There are only two things in this life that are eternal: the Word of God and the souls of man. How you answer this question may also determine what type of women's ministry you want to cultivate. Ministry among women happens along the line as we do life together centered on the truth of God's Word. It should be oriented around end-of-the-line thinking and living. It is leading women in light of eternity.

The Word of God was written by forty different writers, in three languages over 1500 years, and yet it is one cohesive story. The fourth question of the *Westminster Larger Catechism* asks: "How doth it appear that the Scriptures are the Word of God?" The answer to the question is: "The Scriptures manifest themselves to be the Word of God, by their majesty and purity; by the consent of all the parts, and the scope of the whole, which is to give all glory to God . . ." This consent and scope principle of Scripture applies to every part of our lives—our chief end is to glorify God. We are a product of our theology. What we believe about God is reflected in our words, actions, and attitudes. When a woman's theology is fragmented, her life may be incoherent and disjointed. She is living for ephemeral dots and does not understand how all these parts fit together. However, just as every part of Scripture agrees perfectly with every other part, every part or dot in a woman's life has meaning and significance. In His sovereignty, God aligns the parts of her life to agree with the whole of His purpose for His glory. Biblically speaking, there are no random dots. Nothing in God's economy is wasted. He uses every relationship, circumstance, and event in our lives for us to ". . . be conformed to the image of his Son" (Rom. 8:29). Women's ministry operates with clarity and cohesion along the line when this truth undergirds all we do.

We must always remember that life and ministry along the line is only possible in the Spirit. Paul encourages us, "If we live by the Spirit, let us also keep in step with the Spirit" (Gal. 5:25). Every step a woman takes towards eternity is Spirit-empowered. Mission and mandate are two of the scriptural guardrails that keep us moving toward the desired destination.

The mission begins in a Garden and will end in a City. "And God blessed them. And God said to them, 'Be fruitful and multiply and fill the earth and subdue it, and have dominion over the fish of the sea and over the birds of the heavens and over every living thing that moves on the earth'" (Gen. 1:28). The mission of image-bearers is to spread Eden to the ends of the earth. Multiplication and fruitfulness will be both biological and spiritual. Because of the fall, we deserved death and fruitlessness, but instead, we were given the promise of Life through a Redeemer (Gen. 3:15). After the fall, Adam's authority to express dominion and name the creatures was restored because of the gospel promise. In response, Adam gave his wife a new name that sounds like the Hebrew word for "life" or "life-giver": Eve (Gen. 3:20). Her capacity for biological and spiritual fruitfulness was restored.

The Cultural Mandate and the Great Commission go hand in hand. "Go therefore and make disciples of all nations, baptizing them in the name of the Father and of the Son and of the Holy Spirit, teaching them to observe all that I have commanded you. And behold, I am with you always, to the end of the age" (Matt. 28:19-20). We are called to go and show the life-giving hope of the gospel. Women's ministry holds the potential to show it as both believable and beautiful. Everywhere we go along the line we have the opportunity to sow gospel seeds in faith, praying disciples might grow. Women's ministry is teaching "all He has commanded" (Word-based) to Christ's disciples (relationally-driven). We are encouraged to persevere in the power of His presence because He will be with us to the "end of the age"— the end of the mission.

Titus 2 echoes the cultural and gospel mandates, showing that some discipleship is gender-specific: "But as for you, teach what accords with sound doctrine. . . . Older women likewise are to be reverent in behavior, not slanderers or slaves to much wine. They are to teach what is good, and so train the young women to love their husbands and children, to be self-controlled, pure, working at home, kind, and submissive to their own husbands, that the word of God may not be reviled. . . . but showing all good faith, so that in everything they may adorn the doctrine of God our Savior" (Titus 2:1, 3-5, 10). This passage is not about building strong women, but rather a strong church. Its aim is teaching women to think and live biblically in the context of the Church because we will do it for eternity. Christ is preparing the Church as His Bride to look more and more like Him. Preparation involves Christ's redemption on the cross and His sanctification by the Spirit. One of the tools the Spirit may also use is His women engaged in kingdom discipleship, preparing the Bride to bring all of life under the rule and reign of King Jesus.

Investing in the life of another woman is a sacred and life-giving calling. The word "sound" informs our methods and motivations for women's ministry. It means "healthy or hygienic." It is robust, strong, whole, full of life, thriving, and flourishing. Women's ministry must be Word-based (sound doctrine) and relationally-driven (older women and younger women in a discipleship relationship with one another). Sound living, sound relationships, sound women's ministry, and a sound church flow out of the teaching of sound doctrine. Spiritual mothers are called to walk out the content of the gospel in the context of their relationships with their spiritual daughters for the glory of God. It is God's strategy to train the next generation of women to live and lead in light of eternity. Titus 2 relationships put the gospel on display to a watching world. They highlight the enduring truth of His Word, so no one will malign or defame it. "The grass withers, the flower fades, but the word of our God will stand forever" (Isa. 40:8).

This book is filled with women who are living and leading along the line. These women are just like you. They all struggle to believe what is true and are easily distracted with "dot-type" pursuits. Be encouraged though, because these women are fellow pilgrims seeking to be led by the Spirit, to live by the Spirit, and to keep in step with the Spirit (Gal. 5:16-26). They are spiritual mothers who will show you the shape of godliness in their words. They are fellow women's ministry leaders investing in the eternal things: the Word of God and the souls of women. They are gospel friends whose aim is to apply the content of the gospel in the context of their relationships. Their eyes are fixed on the destination, and they will keep praying and walking until they get Home. It is my prayer that the truths contained in this book will help your women's ministry equip the women in your church to think and live biblically in the context of the church community. Come and let's walk the line together.

Karen Hodge is the Coordinator of Women's Ministry in the Presbyterian Church in America (PCA) and is the co-author of *Transformed: Life-taker to Life-giver* and *Life-giving Leadership*.

Part One

Foundations of a Discipleship Ministry

Chapter 1

Is God's Word Distracting You?
Pey Chu

We live in a cultural moment in which we're attuned to what we eat. One hardly needs to look further than the proliferation of diets that claim not only to help you shed a few pounds but promise better all-around health: gluten-free diets, ketogenic diets, vegetarian and vegan diets, and the list goes on. Even fast food restaurants, never the paragon of healthful eating, commonly list calorie counts next to menu items. As new information emerges about the health benefits of kale (or whatever the latest wonder food is), we flock to the grocery store to buy it in bulk. Stand around long enough listening to a group of women talking and you will likely hear about what one person is choosing to eat or not to eat. The reason we're paying attention to what we eat is because we realize that what we eat affects our health.

Given our cultural sensitivities, we should be well equipped to appreciate the significance of Jesus' words: "Man shall not live by bread alone, but by every word that comes from the mouth of God" (Matt. 4:4). Just as food sustains and nourishes physical life, so too God's Word sustains and nourishes spiritual life. Our souls' need for God and His life-giving words equals and eclipses our bodies' need for food. But as much as we are attuned to the physical truth, we seem to be blind to the spiritual truth. We are quick to tell other women what wonderful free-range, organic, gluten-free, sugar-free, non-GMO lollipop we found at the local Trader Joe's, but are we as quick to share nuggets of spiritual sustenance that we have found?

Imagine, for example, that 21 percent of people claimed that eating food was unimportant to physical life, and that another 37 percent of people claimed it wasn't an essential part of human life. Such is the spiritual state of evangelicalism. In a recent Pew Research survey, only 42 percent of Christians believed that reading the Bible was an essential part of being a Christian.[1] It would be ludicrous to say that only 58 percent of Christians believe that eating food is essential for life. Yet that is the state of our spiritual health. We are facing a spiritual famine, and women's ministry leaders must help the women in our church address the need for spiritual aid.

In 1879, Charles Spurgeon offered these words:

You know how necessary it is that we should be fed upon the truth of Holy Scripture . . . I am afraid that this is a magazine-reading age, a newspaper-reading age, a periodical-reading age, but not so much a Bible-reading age as it ought to be . . . You shall find that reading the Word of God for yourselves, reading it rather than notes upon it, is the surest way of growing in grace.[2]

Though well over a century old, Spurgeon's words are still relevant today. Magazines, newspapers, and periodicals have been replaced with blogs, newsfeeds, and tweets. Are these leading us to grow in grace as found in the gospel of Christ? We live in a technological era where our buffet of distractions is bountiful and plenteous. The smartphones in our purses put a world of information at our fingertips, providing us with a never-ending stream of beeps and vibrations. The medium for distraction may be different, but the problem is age-old.

We must ask ourselves what it is that we spend our time reading and ingesting. What are the influences that speak to us? Is it Facebook updates, click bait, email, or Amazon reviews? Why do we spend time reading and pondering the things that we do? Are we committed to reading and spending time in the Word of God with the same consistency, frequency, and fervor as checking Instagram and Pinterest posts? There is a battle for our hearts and minds, and today's Christian woman is in danger of being woefully unprepared. We must allow God's Word to define every part of our being.

The issue isn't merely distraction, however. It is that the information and opinions we absorb shape our beliefs and convictions. There are no brute, uninterpreted facts, yet we often lack a grasp of biblical doctrines that would allow us to discern where the facts at hand have been spun in an unbiblical direction. From our cultural consensus on issues of morality to pop psychology's account of who we are and what ails us to the received wisdom of the academy, we are bombarded with a dizzying array of half-truths and outright lies. Considering this background, we cannot afford to have a weak understanding of Scripture. When we uncritically accept what the world throws at us without examining the underlying presuppositions and follow those presuppositions to their sometimes-pernicious conclusions, we are courting disaster.

It is therefore imperative for us to have a robust view of Scripture in order to be able to sniff out imitation gospels while developing a more discerning palate for the authentic. In this digital age, anyone can blog, anyone can have a podcast, anyone can be a YouTube star, anyone can write and anyone can get published.[3] Celebrity Christians, the blogosphere, social media influencers, and self-help gurus too often are being afforded functional authority in our lives over and against the wisdom found in the Word of God. We must be more discerning and biblically-rooted. Christ in us gives us our wisdom and confidence in the supremacy of His Word. Only as we dig into God's Word can we make true sense of the world around us and find what our hearts long for.

In Paul's second letter to Timothy, he warns, "But understand this, that in the last days there will come times of difficulty" (2 Tim. 3:1). Then he lists a series of issues—issues similar to what we still face today. The solution for Timothy in dealing with these difficulties is found a few verses later:

. . . you have been acquainted with the sacred writings, which are able to make you wise for salvation through faith in Christ Jesus. All Scripture is breathed out by God and profitable for teaching, for reproof, for correction, and for training

in righteousness, that the man of God may be competent,
equipped for every good work (2 Tim. 3:15-17).

The sacred writings' goal is faith in Christ. God has breathed
out the Scriptures, and they are profitable. They not only
make Timothy (and us) wise for salvation, but in Scripture,
we find God's words equipping us for maturity. Too often, we
want to treat the Bible as an encyclopedia or cookbook. For
example, if we cannot find a verse about eating disorders, then
we think surely Scripture is silent about this topic, and we are
unable to help our friend in need. Or we assume that since
we have added all the right ingredients together, we are now
entitled to a delectable dish of ease and prosperity served up
by God Himself. God's Word offers us so much more, and we
must become thoughtful students of His Word.

Theologians often talk about four attributes of Scripture:
sufficiency, authority, necessity, and clarity (perspicuity).
As 21st century women, understanding these attributes will
safeguard us from becoming cultural lemmings. Knowing
these attributes and applying them to our view of Scripture
will prepare us to engage wisely with the issues around us.
Pastor and author Kevin DeYoung unpacks the attributes of
the Word of God this way: "Each of the attributes . . . is meant
to protect an important truth about the Bible. . . . [W]e could
say: 'God's word is final; God's word is understandable; God's
word is necessary; and God's word is enough.'"[4]

The sufficiency of God's Word means that we do not need
to seek out something more modern or relevant to speak to
us. In our current usage, "sufficient" can have the connotation
of being merely adequate, but that's not the sense in which
Scripture is sufficient. Rather, the idea is that everything
we need to bring us unto salvation and mature us in Christ,
God has given us in His Word. "His divine power has granted
to us all things that pertain to life and godliness, through
the knowledge of him who called us to his own glory and
excellence" (2 Peter 1:3).

Several years ago, a devotional book came out capturing
the attention of many women. It seemed to be everywhere,
on bookshelves, on nightstands, even reaching us overseas

in Asia on the mission field. The book seeks to encourage believers toward a closer relationship with God by imagining a fresh dialogue with Jesus. But the essence of the book is problematic because the desire to hear from God beyond Scripture implies that God's words to us in Scripture are in some way lacking. This prompted many in evangelical circles to warn readers about the book.[5] Despite these warnings, the book's popularity has not slowed as evidenced by its many offshoots. This popularity is just one example of an anemic view of the sufficiency of the Word of God. Women in our churches are quick to jump on spiritual bandwagons without engaging more deeply in Scripture itself.

God's Word is authoritative. We must allow the Word of God to dictate our moral views. Just as His Word is sufficient for us in our spiritual life, it is also authoritative in how we live our physical lives. To allow the Word of God to have authority in our lives is to give authority to God Himself. Theologian Wayne Grudem says, "All the words in Scripture are God's words in such a way that to disbelieve or disobey any word of Scripture is to disbelieve or disobey God."[6] When I write a note to my child instructing him to empty the dishwasher, he had better empty that dishwasher! Ignoring the note and claiming that I had not personally spoken those words to him and, besides, he didn't really feel like it, will not excuse his disobedience. The authority in that note is an extension of my authority over him as his parent. God's words to us in Scripture show us how to "walk in a manner worthy of the Lord, fully pleasing to him" (Col. 1:10).

In recent Internet history, a Christian blogger became a celebrity through the world of social media. She was engaging. She was current. She was relevant. She cared about social justice. She was real. She was funny. Then, she revealed that her views on marriage are anything but biblical. Rather, they are another manifestation of secular culture bleeding into sound Christian doctrine. Unfortunately, this has not hindered Christians in the social media world from continuing to share her posts and link to her blogs. We must stand firm on the authority of the Word of God, lest we also float along with the winds of change, declaring God-ordained marriage to be between anyone who claims to love each other. The commands of God are not mere suggestions that we accept only if the mood hits or if the culture allows. We must maintain a lofty view of the authority of Scripture to avoid being dragged away by an avalanche of social pressure.

As the Word of God is authoritative in directing our lives, the clarity of Scripture informs us how our lives are to be directed. This attribute of the Word of God helps us see, with the Holy Spirit enlightening us, that Scripture is clear. Early 20th century Dutch theologian Herman Bavinck makes this helpful distinction: "This does not mean that the Bible is so transparent as to need no interpretation. . . . [Clarity] does not mean that there are no mysteries or difficult passages in Scripture. What [clarity] means is that the path of salvation is clearly taught and explained."[7] The Bible is clear on what we need to know for salvation and finding life in Christ.

As 21st century women who have found life in Christ, the necessity of the Word of God in our lives seems ever more urgent. We need the rich words of Scripture to inform our views of God (theology), our understanding of man (anthropology), and our understanding of our need for salvation through Christ (soteriology). Scripture is necessary to expose our darkened hearts, to understand our need for life through Christ, and to guide us in living in a manner that is pleasing to Him. Without Scripture, we fumble around with the rest of the world, making vain attempts at finding purpose. We are desperate to understand who we are given how many personality tests are on web pages: Which Disney Princess are you? Which Harry Potter character would you be? Pick your favorite 80s songs, and we'll tell you how you like your steak cooked. We want to know, but we can't know rightly unless we are settled in the steady, unchanging Word of God.

There is a plea in Proverbs that we "be attentive to my words; incline your ear to my sayings. Let them not escape from your sight; keep them within your heart. For they are life to those who find them, and healing to all their flesh" (Prov. 4:20-22). God's Word brings us life and healing. Are we rooting ourselves in this Word to find life and healing for our souls? Or do we seek the temporary balm of shared experiences to soothe our hearts and hurts? Do we run to and "long for the pure spiritual milk, that by it [we] may grow up to salvation" (1 Peter 2:2)? Are we growing and maturing "so that we may no longer be children, tossed to and fro by the waves and carried about by every wind of doctrine, by human cunning, by craftiness in deceitful schemes" (Eph. 4:14)? Are we equipping ourselves with a rich understanding of Scripture in order to navigate the waves of life and culture?

If we are to grow in grace, we need to go to the source of grace. We do not read the Bible just to be able to feel a sense of accomplishment by checking off a box on our reading plan. Reading plans and check lists are helpful, but we read the Bible ultimately to see and know the God of the Bible. We read the Bible to find the Christ to whom the stories point. We read the Bible and understand it as the Holy Spirit illuminates it for us. We must study the Bible. Over the years, I have been in several "Bible studies" that functioned more like book clubs. Rather than study Scripture, we would read a book about a Christian topic and discuss it. Clearly, I am not saying that there is no value in reading Christian books (you are reading one right now) or discussing relevant topics. There definitely is a place for rich books on our bookshelves. I am trying to point out that often we throw in the Bible as just another side dish of readings. We can take it or leave it or use it when it suits us, sprinkling a verse here or there as a little seasoning. However, in order for us to grow in true grace, the Bible must be the main meal upon which we feed. It won't do to snack our way through life. Women's ministry leaders ought to make every effort to see that those under their care are getting a steady diet of life-giving nourishment.

Months ago, a woman came to me for counsel. She was facing some struggles in her life and was spiraling into depression. She had been praying for answers, but God was silent. She didn't feel Him responding to her and she felt as if God had abandoned her in her time of need. I asked her what parts of Scripture had been a beacon of light to her in the dark moments. She confessed that she had not been reading Scripture. What if in her sadness, she had camped out in the Word of God? Perhaps she would have been led to God's numerous promises that "He will be with you; he will not leave you or forsake you. Do not fear or be dismayed" (Deut. 31:8). Maybe these words of promise could have given her hope in her situation. God seemed silent to her because she was not availing herself of the means that God has given us to hear His voice. I do not want to minimize the real emotions that she had and the real sadness that she felt, but our real emotions and our real sadness can be touched by a very real Christ who comforts us. We find this Christ in the Scriptures. God's perceived silence can be broken when we take the time to hear Him through His words in the Holy Scriptures.

Too many mistakenly believe that God speaks to us in some mystical way, but meeting with God doesn't have to happen in some spiritual-mountain-top moment. It can come from a very mundane, Tuesday-morning reading of Scripture. God can do extraordinary things in us through the ordinary study of His Word. I often hear people saying that they don't "feel" Him speaking. We may not demand that He speak audibly to us, but we demand that He "speak to my heart." The problem is that "The heart is deceitful above all things, and desperately sick; who can understand it" (Jer. 17:9)? Our emotions cannot be trusted to be the final arbiter of truth. Scripture is our only authority for interpreting the world around us. Scripture has to inform and shape us.

Recently, I read about a concept of raising girls and boys as "theybies." It appears that a few parents are raising their children without assigning them a gender. These children are called "they" and are encouraged to decide later for themselves what gender they would like to be.[8] The physical gender assigned by God in our creation design (Gen. 1-2) is rejected. Our culture today is denying that the God who, "In the beginning, . . . created the heavens and the earth [is also the God who created them] male and female he created them" (Gen. 1:1, 27). For those without the Holy Spirit and the Word of God in their lives, this is the best that can be done to make sense of the world. It isn't only confusion about gender; it is confusion about the very core of who we are. But for those of us who have faith in Jesus Christ as our Savior, we find definition, sanity and hope. Hebrews 1:1-4 says this:

Long ago, at many times and in many ways, God spoke to our fathers by the prophets, but in these last days he has spoken to us by his Son, whom he appointed the heir of all things, through whom also he created the world. He is the radiance of the glory of God and the exact imprint of his nature, and he upholds the universe by the word of his power. After making purification for sins, he sat down at the right hand of the Majesty on high, having become as much superior to angels as the name he has inherited is more excellent than theirs.

God has spoken to us through His Son. The gospel of Jesus Christ not only brings us to faith in Him, but it also perfects us in Him. The gospel is counterintuitive and countercultural. We need the corrective lens of Scripture again and again to bring us back to viewing all of life correctly. We need daily to hear Christ's voice speaking gospel truths to us in Scripture. We need regularly to be convicted of our deep depravity, selfishness, and rebellion, and at the same time to be shown the grace of God in the face of Christ. We find these truths and this grace in the sufficient, authoritative, clear, and necessary Word of God.

Pey Chu (MDiv in Counseling, Westminster Theological Seminary, PA) is a pastor's wife, a mom, a counselor and a former foreign missionary.

DISCUSSION QUESTIONS

1. What are the constant distractions that pull women away from truly studying and engaging in God's Word? What are some practical steps to connect women to Scripture?

2. How does understanding the attributes of Scripture (authority, necessity, clarity, and sufficiency) help women to navigate the world and culture around them? Are women biblically literate?

3. In what way do you see Christ at work in your life as you interact with a higher view of Scripture?

1 Abigail Geiger, "5 facts on how Americans view the Bible and other religious texts," http://www.pewresearch.org/fact-tank/2017/04/14/5-facts-on-how-americans-view-the-bible-and-other-religious-texts/.

2 Charles H. Spurgeon, "How to Read the Bible," http://www.bible-researcher.com/spurgeon2.html.

3 The irony is not lost on me that I also fit into this category.

4 Kevin DeYoung, *Taking God at His Word: Why the Bible Is Knowable, Necessary, and Enough, and What That Means for You and Me* (Wheaton, IL: Crossway, 2014), 44-45.

5 "Developing Discernment in Devotional Reading," *Christian Research Journal*, Volume 38, No. 4, https://www.equip.org/article/developing-discernment-devotional-reading/.

6 Wayne Grudem, *Systematic Theology: An Introduction to Biblical Doctrine* (Grand Rapids, MI: Zondervan Publishing House, 1994), 73.

7 Herman Bavinck, *Reformed Dogmatics*, vol. 1, *Prolegomena*, ed. John Bolt, trans. John Vriend (Grand Rapids, MI: Baker Academic, 2003), 450.

8 Alex Morris, "It's a Theyby!" *New York Magazine*, April 2, 2018, https://www.thecut.com/2018/04/theybies-gender-creative-parenting.html.

Chapter 2

Covenant Theology: A Theological and Gospel Foundation for Women's Ministry
Sarah Ivill

T he study of covenant theology needs to be rediscovered among women in the Church today. Where its teaching in women's ministry flourishes, the gospel flourishes. Where it is appreciated and understood by women, joy-filled worship, generous work for the glory of God, and bold witnessing of the gospel of Christ ensue. C. H. Spurgeon says that, "He who understands the covenant has reached the very core and marrow of the gospel."[1] J. I. Packer says, "In modern Christendom, covenant theology has been unjustly forgotten."[2] He claims that the gospel of God, the Word of God, and the reality of God are not properly understood until they are viewed in a covenantal framework.[3]

WHAT IS COVENANT THEOLOGY?
Theologian J. I. Packer defines it as "what is nowadays called a hermeneutic—that is, a way of reading the whole Bible that is itself part of the overall interpretation of the Bible that it undergirds. A successful hermeneutic is a consistent interpretive procedure yielding a consistent understanding of Scripture that in turn confirms the propriety [correctness] of the procedure itself."[4] When properly understood, covenant theology is synonymous with Reformed theology. It is not a theological system that we impose on Scripture but a framework inherent in Scripture. It is God's own way of revealing Himself from Genesis to Revelation with Christ as the center of the covenant story. Scripture is clear that God condescended to man by way of covenant. In fact, the relationship between the three persons of the Godhead is

covenantal. Furthermore, His revelation to us is a covenant book. Whenever we study any passage of Scripture then, we should be thinking covenantally.

WHAT IS COVENANT?

Covenant is God's sovereign initiation to have a binding relationship with His people, grounded in His grace and promises, and secured by His own blood.[5] Scripture reveals four main ideas regarding the concept of covenant. First, it involves God's presence. God initiated a relationship with His creatures in which He committed to be their God and dwell among them, "I will be your God and you will be my people" (Gen. 17:7-8; Ex. 6:7; Lev. 26:12; Jer. 32:38; Ezek. 14:11; Zech. 8:8; 2 Cor. 6:16; Heb. 8:10; Rev. 21:3). His presence, protection and promises are intricately related and rooted in His loyal lovingkindness. Second, it involves the person of Christ. After His resurrection Jesus taught His disciples that He is the center of the covenant story and the One that holds the story together (Luke 24:44). Third, it involves the people of God. God has sovereignly and lovingly chosen a people for Himself, not because they merit His favor, but because of His covenantal lovingkindness. Finally, the concept of covenant includes the practice of God's people. Just as the characteristics of God's covenant are relational, familial, corporate, generational, and compassionate, so our ministries are to be.

HOW IS THE BIBLE A COVENANT BOOK?

In order to understand how the entirety of Scripture is covenantal, we can take a close look at Deuteronomy. During Moses' day the idea of covenant was familiar. The ancient Near East had developed suzerain-vassal treaties, and the Hittite treaties (1450-1180 BC) are remarkably similar to what we find in Scripture. These treaties were between a suzerain (the great king) and a vassal (the lesser king), and they were meant to provide protection for the vassal and his people. The great king would protect the vassal from enemies and the vassal, as well as his people, would obey the suzerain. These treaties involved deep affections since the great king was rescuing the vassal from danger as a father rescues a son. This meant the vassal and his people were to both love and obey the suzerain.[6]

These treaties involved several elements. The *preamble*
stated the name of the great king who was making the treaty.
The *historical prologue* stated the gracious and merciful rescue
of the vassal by the suzerain, forming both the backbone of
the treaty and the reason the vassal should obey and love him.
The *stipulations* were the rules that rendered the people either
covenant-keepers or covenant-breakers and were accompanied
by an appeal to witnesses to testify for or against them,
depending on their faithfulness or unfaithfulness. The *sanctions*
explained what would occur if the people broke the covenant,
such as exile, and included the blessings and curses that would
fall upon covenant-keepers or covenant-breakers, respectively.
There were also *tablets inscribed with the treaty* that were
kept in both parties' temples, regular readings of it so that each
generation knew the requirements, and public ceremonies to
ratify the treaty, the latter of which included both parties passing
between animals that had been cut in two as if to say—If I fail to
uphold my part of the treaty, you may do to me as has been done
to these animals.[7]

Deuteronomy begins with the covenant speaker (1:1-5),
moves to the covenant story (1:6-4:43), then to the covenant
stipulations (4:44-26:19), and sanctions (27:1-30:20), before
closing with the covenant succession (31-34). This covenantal
pattern is found in Scripture as a whole. The Lord God is
the Great King who has lovingly condescended to protect,
provide for and preserve His people. The redemptive story
displays why we owe Him our love and loyalties. The covenant
stipulations are spelled out throughout Scripture, and we see
the covenant sanctions occur at many different points of the
covenant story. For example, Adam and Eve are banished from
the Garden of Eden, the wicked are destroyed through the
flood, and Israel is exiled from the land.

KEY BIBLICAL COVENANTS
In order to better grasp the covenantal structure of Scripture,
we need to study the covenant of redemption, the covenant of
works, and the covenant of grace. Jesus, addressing the crowds
and claiming that He is the Bread of Life, said, "All that the

Father gives me will come to me, and whoever comes to me I will never cast out. For I have come down from heaven, not to do my own will but the will of him who sent me . . . that I should lose nothing of all that he has given me, but raise it up on the last day" (John 6:37-39; see also 10:25-29; 17:1-10). This agreement—that the Father would send His Son into the world in order to lose none of the people He has given Him—took place before the foundation of the world, as is confirmed by the apostle Paul's words in Ephesians 1:3-4, "Blessed be the God and Father of our Lord Jesus Christ, who has blessed us in Christ with every spiritual blessing in the heavenly places, even as he chose us in him before the foundation of the world . . ." The *covenant of redemption* between the triune God, as revealed in Scripture, teaches that the Father purposed our redemption, the Son accomplished it, and the Holy Spirit applies it. This covenant is foundational to the covenant of grace, which we will look at below.

But first, we need to understand the *covenant of works*. In Genesis 1-2, we learn that God's relationship with creation is covenantal. As Michael Horton says, "The pattern of creation, after all, is covenantal: the Great King speaks and the servant (stars, wind, land animals, birds, fish, mountains, rivers, oceans, and finally this marvel of ensouled dust, Adam) answers back faithfully. 'Let there be . . . !' And there was . . .' This also fits the pattern of treaty making. The great king would decree the terms of the treaty, and the servant would reply, 'Here I am.'"[8] He goes on to say, "The covenant is always the site where the Great King and his servants are recognized for what they are: unequal partners with their own way of existing, knowing, willing, and acting—one as Creator, the other as creature."[9]

So, in the beginning Adam was in a covenantal relationship with God and was free to respond to the Great King with either obedience or disobedience.

Although Adam had the capability not to sin, he also had the capability to sin. He was a free agent who could choose how to respond to the King. God clearly set forth covenantal elements in His relationship with Adam. Adam was to worship God, work for His glory, join with the woman God gave him to multiply and fill the earth with offspring, and he was to do all this under the authority of God's word. The penalty for disobeying the King would be death.

We learn from Romans 5 that Adam was the federal head of the entire human race, representing all humanity. When he failed to obey God's word not to eat from the Tree of the Knowledge of Good and Evil, all mankind fell with him in that first transgression and became covenant-breakers. " . . . just as sin came into the world through one man, and death through sin, and so death spread to all men because all sinned—for sin indeed was in the world before the law was given, but sin is not counted where there is no law. Yet death reigned from Adam to Moses, even over those whose sinning was not like the transgression of Adam, who was a type of the one who was to come" (Rom. 5:12-14). The antitype is Christ, who has made all God's people righteous as the second Adam, who perfectly obeyed the law on our behalf (active obedience) and took the curse of God upon Himself for our sin (passive obedience). When Adam and Eve disobeyed the King, they received covenant curses but embedded in the curses was some wonderful news.

The first glimpse of the gospel in Scripture occurs in Genesis 3:15, "I will put enmity between you and the woman, and between your offspring and her offspring; he shall bruise your head, and you shall bruise his heel." Although the word *covenant* is not used in Genesis 3, the entire structure of these opening chapters is clearly covenantal and should be seen as the beginning point of the *covenant of grace* in Scripture, which "was made with Christ as the second Adam, and in him with all the elect as his seed."[10] The covenant of grace includes God's postfall covenants with Adam, Noah, Abraham, Moses, and David, as well as the new covenant that progressively reveal the one overarching covenant of grace, which rests on the foundation of the covenant of redemption. God's covenant with Adam included the curse of sorrow and struggle for Eve, as well as her daughters (all women throughout all generations), with regard to childbearing and marriage. But it also included the blessing of reproducing seed, which eventually would culminate in Christ. Adam received the curse of sweaty toil and the separation of body and soul at death, but inherent in these curses was also a blessing—he would receive sustenance from the Lord. He would still work and he would still live, but his work would be hard, and he wouldn't live forever. Adam and Eve's exile from the Garden of Eden was in true covenant form. It was one of the sanctions for not obeying the stipulations of the treaty, but even in the face of exile lay the hope of restoration. The cherubim and flaming sword that guarded the way to the Tree of Life would one day be removed by the second Adam, Jesus Christ, "who has passed through the heavens" and "who in every respect has been tempted as we are, yet without sin" so that we can "with confidence draw near to the throne of grace, that we may receive mercy and find grace to help in time of need" (Heb. 4:14-16).

God's covenant with Noah is the next progressive revelation of God's covenant of grace (Gen. 8:20-9:17). Immediately preceding this covenant is the story of the flood in which God saves a remnant (Noah and his family) from His judgment through the ark, which anticipates the greater work of Christ saving God's people from judgment through the cross. In His covenant with Noah, God promises His glorious grace alongside His glorious justice. We see the former in the fact that "While the earth remains, seedtime and harvest, cold and heat, summer and winter, day and night, shall not cease" (8:22). We see the latter in the fact that "From his fellow man I will require a reckoning for the life of man" (9:5). There is also a genealogical aspect to the covenant, "I establish my covenant with you and your offspring after you" (9:9). We also see God's promise of the goodness of life and general grace extended to all mankind, "never again shall there be a flood to destroy the earth" (9:11). The sign of the covenant is the bow in the cloud. Some see this as a bow with an arrow pointing up at heaven to pierce the Son of God; others see it as a rainbow in the sky in the midst of stormy clouds of judgment. Regardless, it proclaims the message that alongside God's judgment stands God's grace. This of course is most fully revealed in His Son Jesus Christ. "And the Word became flesh and dwelt among us, and we have seen his glory, glory as of the only Son from the Father, full of grace and truth" (John 1:14).

God's covenant with Abraham included the promise of

God's presence, a great people who would come through his seed, the possession of the land of promise, and a purpose that was far greater than Abraham could imagine—all the families of the earth would be blessed through his family line (Gen. 15). The passage, strange as it may seem to our ears, is a perfect example of the treaties that occurred during the time Moses was writing the Pentateuch. It was customary in the treaty-making process to cut animals in half and have each party walk through them in order to commit to the terms of the treaty. In essence, the parties were saying to each other, "Just as these animals have been cut in two, so let it be done to me if I break my covenant commitment." God's covenant with Abraham was strikingly different from other treaties of the day in one way. It was unheard of that one of the parties wouldn't walk through the cut animals, and yet this is exactly what happened in God's covenant with Abraham. The smoking fire pot and flaming torch, which symbolized God, passed between the cut pieces, but Abraham did not. This covenant of promise is a beautiful foreshadowing of the Lamb of God who takes away the sin of the world. It would be God who kept both parties' promises. Jesus is both the Lord of the covenant, extending grace and peace to covenant-breakers, and the servant of the covenant, perfectly fulfilling what God's people could not fulfill.

God's covenant with Moses and Israel is the next progressive unfolding of God's covenant of grace and can best be summarized by the Ten Commandments (Ex. 20:1-17; Deut. 5:6-21). The prologue, "I am the LORD your God, who brought you out of the land of Egypt, out of the house of slavery" (Ex. 20:2; Deut. 5:6), is important to keep in mind as we consider whether this covenant is a further revelation of the covenant of grace (as I contend), or a covenant that stands in sharp distinction from the covenant of promise with Abraham (as some theologians contend).[11] It should not be surprising that God would give His people, who were now in the form of a theocratic nation, commandments to live by. He was the Great King, and they were His people that should be affectionately devoted to Him as their protector and provider. He had already saved them from Egypt; now He wanted them to know how to live in a relationship with Him founded on His covenantal lovingkindness. This covenant with Moses anticipated Christ, the final and perfect mediator and the One who has fulfilled the law perfectly on our behalf. The law reveals we are covenant-breakers in need of a covenant-keeper, and indeed we have one in Jesus Christ.

God's covenant with David is the next progressive unfolding of the covenant of grace in Scripture (2 Sam. 7). God promised David a position (he would be king on the throne in Israel); a place (he would reign in Jerusalem); peace (King David's and Solomon's reigns enjoyed a time of peace in Israel); and progeny (there would be an eternal Davidic king on the throne). Matthew makes it clear that Jesus Christ is the final Davidic king by opening his gospel with, "The book of the genealogy of Jesus Christ, the son of David" (Matt. 1:1). Peter's sermon at Pentecost further confirms Christ is the fulfillment of God's covenant with David, "Being therefore a prophet, and knowing that God had sworn with an oath to him that he would set one of his descendants on his throne, he [David] foresaw and spoke about the resurrection of the Christ, that he was not abandoned to Hades, nor did his flesh see corruption (see Acts 2:25-28 quoting Ps. 16:8-11). This Jesus God raised up, and of that we all are witnesses" (Acts 2:30-32).

The final and climactic unfolding of the covenant of grace in Scripture is the new covenant (Jer. 31:31-34). In this covenant God promises His people several things: a return to the land; a restoration of the land; a realization of all the previous promises made with David, Moses, Abraham, Noah, and Adam; renewed hearts; a removal of sin; the reunion of Israel and Judah under one ruler; and the realization of redemption, the latter of which ensures this is the final and climactic covenant.

In light of the unfolding of the covenant of grace in the Old Testament, it is extremely significant that Jesus defines His own death in covenantal terms. During the last Passover meal, which was also the first Lord's Supper, Jesus told His disciples, "This cup that is poured out for you is the new covenant in my blood" (Luke 22:20). In other words, the new covenant is fulfilled through the death of Christ. Through His death, which culminated in His resurrection and ascension, God's people have inherited far more than the land of Canaan; they have inherited the entire earth, and it will be a completely restored heaven and earth when Christ comes again. Through Christ's death and resurrection all the previous promises made to Adam, Noah, Abraham, Moses, and David were fulfilled (2 Cor. 1:20). God's people were given renewed hearts and a removal of sin; He broke down the wall of hostility between Jews and Gentiles and made "one new man in place of the two" (Eph. 2:15); and He accomplished the redemption of God's people, which He had covenanted to do in the covenant of redemption with the other two persons of the Godhead, the Father and the Holy Spirit.

Covenant theology provides both the context to understand God's unfolding story of redemption and a comprehension of God's covenant with humankind, which in turn deepens our appreciation of our adoption, reminds us of the thanksgiving due His name, and exhorts us toward faithfulness as His people.[12] As women come to a deeper appreciation of it, the result will be joyful worship, generous work for God's glory, and bold witnessing for Christ.

Sarah Ivill (ThM, Dallas Theological Seminary) is a conference speaker and the author of several Bible studies and books, including *The Covenantal Life: Appreciating the Beauty of Theology and Community.*

DISCUSSION QUESTIONS

1. How has this essay challenged you to think about covenant theology as a hermeneutic that you can employ in your women's ministry?

2. How do you see evidence in your women's ministry of:
— covenant theology being appreciated and understood by women?
— joy-filled worship?
— generous work for the glory of God?
— bold witnessing of the gospel of Christ?

3. As you learned about God's covenant with Adam, Noah, Abraham, Moses, and David, as well as the new covenant, several characteristics of the covenant should have come to mind, such as relational, familial, corporate and generational. What implications do these characteristics have for your women's ministry?

4. How has seeing Christ's death in covenantal terms challenged you, comforted you, convicted you, or changed your thinking in some way? How does Christ's death challenge you to humbly help other women in the church?

1   Cited in Peter Golding, *Covenant Theology: The Key of Theology in Reformed Thought and Tradition* (Ross-shire, Great Britain: Christian Focus Publications, 2004), 185.
2   J. I. Packer, Introduction "On Covenant Theology," in *The Economy of the Covenants Between God and Man* by Herman Witsius (Grand Rapids, MI: Reformation Heritage Books, reprinted 2010), 27.
3   Ibid., 31-32, 34.
4   Ibid., 27.
5   Sarah Ivill, *The Covenantal Life: Appreciating the Beauty of Theology and Community* (Grand Rapids: Reformation Heritage Books, 2018), 5.
6   Michael Horton, *God of Promise: Introducing Covenant Theology* (Grand Rapids: Baker Books, 2006), 24-25.
7   Ibid., 25-28.
8   Ibid., 111.
9   Ibid., 112.
10 *Westminster Larger Catechism*, A. 31.
11 I agree with Robertson, "Not only did the covenant of law [God's covenant with Moses] not disannul the covenant of promise [God's covenant with Abraham]; more specifically, it did not offer a temporary alternative to the covenant of promise." O. Palmer Robertson, *The Christ of the Covenants* (Phillipsburg, NJ: P&R Publishing, 1980), 174. For an argument that it is a parenthesis in God's covenant of grace and the Sinaitic covenant is now obsolete see Horton, *God of Promise*, 68-70, 75.
12 Golding, *Covenant Theology*, 185.

Chapter 3

How Recovering a Robust Understanding of Ecclesiology Matters for Ministry
Sarah Ivill

I t is time to recover a robust understanding of the doctrine of the Church. Without it, American evangelicalism is in danger of losing its moorings. Christ did not just come to redeem individuals, He came to redeem a people, and that people is the Church. A women's ministry that tries to function without a proper understanding of the Church will quickly become anemic without the life-giving oxygen of the whole Body. "In recent years, many teachers and preachers have noted that, of all the areas of theology that are most neglected and most misunderstood by the person in the pew, ecclesiology (the doctrine of the Church) is foremost."[1]

Sixteenth-century French Protestant theologian John Calvin, in his famous work *Institutes of the Christian Religion,* writes that the church is that society "into whose bosom God is pleased to gather his sons, not only that they may be nourished by her help and ministry as long as they are infants and children, but also that they may be guided by her motherly care until they mature and at last reach the goal of faith. 'For what God has joined together, it is not lawful to put asunder' (Mark 10:9), so that, for those to whom he is Father the church may also be Mother."[2] Such an important view of the Church has waned among many evangelicals today who place such an emphasis on a personal relationship with Jesus that they neglect the important truth that believers aren't just in a binding relationship with God, but also with God's people. Without a proper understanding of this binding relationship our grasp of the significance of the doctrine of the Church will be far too small.

A BIBLICAL THEOLOGY OF THE CHURCH

"In the beginning, God started a Church. Throughout the Old Testament, He matured her and chastened her. He atoned for her sin through His Son, Jesus Christ. He 'bat mitzvah-ed' her at Pentecost with His Holy Spirit. His angels now roam among all His gathered people, those churches in your town and over the oceans, gathering His elect, completing His Church. One day, He will present her as a spotless bride to His Son, and they will commune for eternity." [3]

The Church is God's special people that He has chosen from before the foundation of the world (Eph. 1) to worship Him, work for His glory, and witness to the nations about Him. "God chooses and preserves for Himself a community elected for eternal life and united by faith, who love, follow, learn from, and worship God together. God sends out this community to proclaim the gospel and prefigure Christ's kingdom by the quality of their life together and their love for one another." [4]

A proper biblical theology of the Church must begin in Genesis. Adam and Eve were the first people in the garden-sanctuary to worship God. After the Fall, we learn that there will be enmity between Satan and "the seed of the woman" (Gen. 3:15), which is not just a person (Christ), but also an entire line (Christ and His Church), the beginnings of this corporate body is seen as early as Genesis 4 when people started to call upon the name of the Lord (v. 26). In Genesis 12-50, the Church takes on a familial form when God calls Abraham and his family to be His people. After the exodus from Egypt, when Israel is assembled at the foot of Mount Sinai, the Lord God, by way of covenant, makes His people a nation (Ex. 19:1-24:18). During the exile, the Church takes the form of a remnant scattered among the nations, and after the exile, the remnant returns to Jerusalem to rebuild the temple and city wall.

In the gospels we learn the New Testament Church will take an even different form and will have both continuity and discontinuity with the Old Testament Church. Regarding continuity, there has always been one people of God saved by grace alone through faith alone. "For although there is a multiple disparity between the church of the Old and New

Testaments as to mode of dispensation, still there is none as to the thing itself. In both was the true church of God, having the same faith, the same hope, and which ought to agree in essentials."[5] Regarding discontinuity, the church is no longer in the form of a nation (Israel), but is a community of those the Lord has chosen to be His and is calling from every tribe, tongue, and nation, to worship Him, work for His glory, and witness for His great name. "[Christ's] church is the true seed of Abraham, the true Israel, the true people of God . . . the true temple of God . . . the true Zion and Jerusalem . . . its spiritual offering, the true religion . . . Nothing of the Old Testament is lost in the New, but everything is fulfilled, matured, has reached its full growth, and now, out of the temporary husk, produces the eternal core."[6]

CHRIST, THE BUILDER

"A doctrine of the church that does not centre on Christ is self-defeating and false. But Jesus said to the disciples who confessed him, 'I will build my church.' To ignore his purpose is to deny his lordship. The good news of Christ's coming includes the good news of what he came to do: to join us to himself and to one another as his body, the new people of God."[7] Not even the gates of hell will prevail against His building campaign (Matt. 16:18). Yet He entrusts a great deal of the work to His people. It is the pastors and elders of the church who are to ensure faithful proclamation of the Word through preaching, administration of the sacraments, and a faithful exercise of discipline (Matt. 16:19). It is the people of the church who are to go and sow the gospel of Christ among all nations, making disciples of all those the Spirit convicts and calls to be the Lord's people (Matt. 28:18-20). Since all authority has already been given to the Son, and He is with us to the end of this age through the ministry of the Holy Spirit, such sowing and reaping is not a possibility but a certainty. The power to accomplish the mission of the church is not in our greatness or giftedness, but in the gift of the Holy Spirit given at Pentecost, which Peter declared was a fulfillment of God's promise (Acts 2:16-21 quoting Joel 2:28-32).

DISTINCTIONS IN DEFINING THE CHURCH

On this side of glory, the Church faces great persecution, seduction, and temptation. It is the Church on earth today (the *Church militant*) that is made up of believers who are pilgrims looking toward the heavenly city where Christ now reigns. Yet, even now we spiritually gather together during corporate worship with the *Church triumphant*, those who have gone before us and are with Jesus in heaven.

The *invisible Church*, which is all God's redeemed people, both past, present, and future, and is only known by God, is the Church "we believe in by faith, the church in communion with God, the church that partakes in all Christ's benefits, the glorious church yet to be fully revealed."[8] We only see the *visible church*, which, though filled with true believers that are also part of the invisible Church, is also filled with those who will one day hear the words, "I never knew you; depart from me" (Matt. 7:23). This helps make sense of the hypocrisy, worldliness, and false teaching in churches today, although it is also true that the fleshly nature that remains in true believers is also partly to blame. The Church is the holy people of God, but not a perfect people. We are saints who still sin while at the same time striving for "peace with everyone, and for the holiness without which no one will see the Lord" (Heb. 12:14).

The Church is both Word-based and relationally driven (see Acts 8:4, 35; 18:28; 28:23, 31). In the context of relationships with others, we faithfully proclaim the kingdom of God and teach about the Lord Jesus Christ by using the Scriptures. As we walk in obedience and humble reliance on the Holy Spirit, the Lord multiplies His Church (Acts 9:31). The Church is to be a holy people, letting her light shine for all to see, so that others can see her good works and glorify the God who saved her (Matt. 5:16).

The New Testament speaks of the *local church*, which highlights the church as an organization in a specific place (see, for example, Acts 8:1; 9:31; 11:26; Rev. 2:1, 8, 12, 18; 3:1, 7, 14). Local churches should always be characterized by the marks of the Church—the Word of God in preaching, administering the sacraments, discipline, and fellowship.

According to the New Testament model, they should be governed by elders, led in service by the diaconate, and filled with committed members that exercise their gifts for the mutual benefit of others while submitting to leadership. "Offices and gifts, governance and the people, organization and organism—all these belong together."[9]

The New Testament also refers to the *Universal Church*, which highlights the Church as an organism that includes believers from all over the world (see Eph. 1:22-23; 4:4-5, 15-16). The universality of the Church leads to its multi-ethnicity, which is rooted in God's covenant with Abraham (see Acts 3:25-26). Jesus called Paul to take the gospel to the Gentiles so that "they may receive forgiveness of sins and a place among those who are sanctified by faith in [Christ]" (Acts 26:18). The Church Triumphant will be filled with a great multitude of worshipers from all tribes, peoples, and languages (Rev. 7:9-10).

IMAGES OF THE CHURCH IN SCRIPTURE

In Genesis 1-2, we first learn of the *garden-city-temple* imagery that becomes interwoven throughout both the Old and New Testaments. In His lovingkindness, the Lord God has chosen to dwell with His creatures. He condescends to their level and initiates a relationship with them. He didn't have to dwell with Adam and Eve in the garden, and He certainly didn't have to give them rules to follow for their good and His glory, but in His lovingkindness He did (Gen. 1:28; 2:16-17). He did the same thing with the nation of Israel by dwelling with them through the tabernacle in the wilderness (Ex. 40:34-38) and then the temple in Jerusalem (1 Kings 6:11-13). The climax of God's presence with His people is found in Christ. At His first coming He tabernacled among mankind, revealing God's glory (John 1:14); at His second coming He will consummately fulfill the promise of God dwelling with His people in the new heaven and earth (Rev. 21:1-22:5).

When God made a covenant with Abraham, He gave him (and his descendants) the sign of circumcision to mark them as *the people of God*. This sign of circumcision became something the Jews were so proud of they couldn't imagine any other ethnic group being part of God's people; in fact, some were tempted to make it a determining factor of salvation (Acts 10:45; 15:1). But Christ "has broken down in his flesh the dividing wall of hostility by abolishing the law of commandments expressed in ordinances, that he might create in himself one new man in place of the two, so making peace, and might reconcile us both to God in one body through the cross" (Eph. 2:14-16). The Greek word for *new* in this context (*kainos*) is not referring to new in origin, but new in quality. In other words, this is not an entirely separate creation from Old Testament Israel, but is related to it just as branches are related to a tree, which is related to the roots (see Rom. 11:11-24).

When the Lord assembled Israel at Mount Zion to make a covenant with them, He defined the Old Testament Church as those people He had delivered from oppression and brought to Himself in order to live a life of obedience as His *treasured possession*, and to be a *kingdom of priests* and a *holy nation* that would cause other nations to see, hear, and revere Him (Ex. 19:4-6; Deut. 4:5-8; Josh. 2:9-11). In the New Testament we learn that Christ, the greater mediator than Moses, has delivered God's people through the second and final exodus on the cross, in which "He disarmed the rulers and authorities and put them to open shame, by triumphing over them in him" (Col. 2:15). Peter picks up the Old Testament description of God's people and applies it to the New Testament Church, "But you are a chosen race, a royal priesthood, a holy nation, a people for his own possession" (1 Peter 2:9). The author to the Hebrews contrasts the people of God at Mount Sinai (Ex. 19) with the New Testament Church at Mount Zion. With the inauguration of Christ's kingdom at His death-resurrection-ascension, believers have already come to "the heavenly Jerusalem, and to innumerable angels in festal gathering, and to the assembly of the firstborn who are enrolled in heaven, and to God, the judge of all, and to the sprits of the righteous made perfect, and to Jesus, the mediator of a new covenant . . . " (Heb. 12:22-24). What the Old Testament prefigured in types and shadows, the New Testament proclaims in its fullness.

The Lord instructed Moses to say to Pharaoh, "Israel is my firstborn son, and I say to you, 'Let my son go that he may serve me'" (Ex. 4:22-23; see also Hos. 11:1). Such *familial language* is also used when the Lord made a covenant with David. In speaking of David's progeny, the Lord said, "I will be to him a father, and he shall be to me a son" (2 Sam. 7:14). This same language is picked up in the New Testament, "For all who are led by the Spirit of God are sons of God. For you did not receive the spirit of slavery to fall back into fear, but you have received the Spirit of adoption as sons, by whom we cry, 'Abba! Father!'" (Rom. 8:14-15).

In 1 Kings 19, we learn that regardless of how small the Old Testament Church might have become at any given time, the Lord still preserved *a remnant* that faithfully worshiped Him. Fleeing Jezebel in fear of his life, Elijah, finding refuge in a cave, met the question of the Lord in the sound of a low whisper, "What are you doing here, Elijah?" (1 Kings 19:13). He replied that the people of Israel had forsaken God's covenant, he alone was left, and they were seeking to kill him (1 Kings 19:14). But the Lord answered that He would leave seven thousand in Israel who had not worshiped Baal (1 Kings 19:18). The Lord always preserves a faithful remnant to worship Him. Paul picks up the storyline of Elijah in Romans 11, "God has not rejected His people whom He foreknew" (11:2), but "at the present time there is a remnant, chosen by grace" (11:5).

In Hosea the Lord uses the imagery of a *husband-wife relationship* to bring judgment against faithless Israel, who has played the whore and has gone after other lovers (Hos. 2:5). The hope of Hosea is that the faithful husband, the Lord God Himself, will love His faithless bride again (Hos. 14:1-9). However, the only way He can take spotted and stained Israel again to Himself is if someone stands in her place and makes her beautiful, indeed, becomes beauty for her. ". . . Christ loved the Church and gave himself up for her, that he might sanctify her, having cleansed her by the washing of water with the word . . ." (Eph. 5:25-26).

In Ezekiel 34, God says, " . . . I myself will search for my sheep and will seek them out . . . And I the LORD, will be their God, and my servant David shall be prince among them. I am the LORD; I have spoken" (Ezek. 34:11, 24). Jesus picks up this *shepherd* imagery when He says, "I am the good shepherd. The good shepherd lays down his life for the sheep" (John 10:11).

No doubt this imagery also lies behind the author's words in the book of Hebrews when he calls Jesus "the great shepherd of the sheep" (Heb. 13:20).

The apostle Paul alone introduces us to the analogy of the church as *the body of Christ* (1 Cor. 12:12, 27; Eph. 1:23; 3:6; 4:4, 12, 16; 5:23, 30; Col. 1:18, 24; 3:15).[10] In Ephesians we learn that after Christ's resurrection and ascension He was given "as head over all things to the church, which is his body, the fullness of him who fills all in all" (Eph. 1:22-23). It is Christ who fills the Church with His power through the promised Holy Spirit so that she becomes what God intends her to be—the spotless bride of Christ who will one day take her place at "the marriage supper of the Lamb" (Rev. 19:9).

THE KINGDOM AND THE CHURCH

When Jesus' disciples asked Him on the day of His ascension if He was restoring the kingdom to Israel, Jesus told them it wasn't for them to know what the Father had fixed by His own authority, and then He gave them another job description. They would be His witnesses over all the earth, empowered by the Holy Spirit (Acts 1:6-8). In other words, it wasn't yet time for Christ to consummate His kingdom that was inaugurated with His life, death, resurrection, and ascension. In the meantime, we are to be witnesses of Christ and His kingdom, which "is where God reigns and His rule is honored and His way of life lived out."[11] The Church heralds the King of the kingdom, proclaiming Christ and Him crucified, and as new converts are made and the Church grows, God's future reign breaks into the present, and the church experiences, in some measure, what the consummated kingdom will be like when God's kingdom will extend over the entirety of the new heaven and earth.[12] Since such an inheritance awaits us, let us be faithful to strive for holiness now, continuing in the faith that has been passed down to us and faithfully passing it to the next generation, not shifting from the hope of the gospel that we have heard proclaimed, and remaining stable and steadfast as we faithfully worship God, work for His glory, and witness for the sake of His great name (Col. 1:21-23; Heb. 12:14).

Sarah Ivill (ThM, Dallas Theological Seminary) is a conference speaker and the author of several Bible studies and books, including *The Covenantal Life: Appreciating the Beauty of Theology and Community.*

DISCUSSION QUESTIONS

1. How would you have defined the Church before reading this essay? How has this essay challenged or confirmed your definition? How does this definition of the Church impact how you do women's ministry?

2. How has this chapter helped you better understand the continuities and discontinuities between the Old Testament Church and the New Testament Church, and how should this affect the way your women's ministry engages in outreach and missions?

3. Briefly describe the different imagery found in Scripture regarding the Church. How have these images helped you have a deeper understanding and better appreciation of the Church, particularly women's ministry? How will they change how you implement ministry, if you're a leader?

4. How can you incorporate regular prayer into your schedule for your pastors, elders, and deacons? Plan to regularly ask your women's ministry leaders how you can be praying for them, and then encourage them by telling them you are.

5. How has this chapter clarified your thinking about the relationship between the kingdom and the Church? How does your women's ministry need to grow in being kingdom-minded?

1   Brian Habig and Les Newsom, *The Enduring Community* (Jackson, MS: Reformed University Press, 2001), 17.

2   John Calvin, *Institutes of the Christian Religion*, ed. John T. McNeill, trans. Ford Lewis Battles (Philadelphia: Westminster, 1960), 4.1.1.

3   Habig and Newsome, *The Enduring Community*, 181.

4   Gospel Coalition and Redeemer Church, *New City Catechism* (Wheaton, IL: Crossway, 2017), 115.

5   Francis Turretin, *Institutes of Elenctic Theology, Vol. 3*, ed., James T. Dennison, Jr., trans., George Musgrave Giger (Philipsburg, NJ: P & R Publishing, 1997), 49.
6   Herman Bavinck, *Reformed Dogmatics*, Volume 3, ed. John Bolt, trans., John Vriend (Grand Rapids, MI: Baker Academic), 224.
7   Edmund P. Clowney, *The Church* (Downers Grove, IL: InterVarsity Press, 1995), 15.
8   Kevin DeYoung and Ted Kluck, *Why We Love the Church* (Chicago, IL: Moody Publishers, 2009), 163.
9   Ibid., 170.
10   Michael Horton, *The Christian Faith: A Systematic Theology for Pilgrims on the Way* (Grand Rapids: Zondervan, 2011), 733.
11   DeYoung and Kluck, *Why We Love the Church*, 39.
12   Wayne Grudem, *Systematic Theology* (Grand Rapids, MI: Zondervan, 1994), 864.

Chapter 4

Image Is Everything:
Women in the Image of God

Vanessa Hawkins

Serving as a Women's Ministry leader, I am frequently invited into the sacred space of hearing my sisters' innermost thoughts and struggles. I have the privilege of hearing the delight and confidence of those who find their value in bearing the image of God and their identity in Christ. I am encouraged and strengthened by those whose lives bear this testimony. But too often I hear women voice deep hurt and brokenness, frustration, confusion and veiled doubt about God's goodness and intentions in creating women. I hear the struggle to fully reconcile biblical truths in light of the multitude of contradictory experiences uninvitedly shaping the lenses through which they see. Now, more than ever, it is necessary that this conversation continues until our views on who women were created to be comes into greater alignment with what Scripture teaches. My hope is to enter that conversation with the express purpose that women see their God with greater clarity and, as a result, know their true value as image-bearers of the Most High God.

CREATION

The notion that humans are made in the image of God, often referred to by the Latin term *Imago Dei,* finds its moorings in the Genesis creation account in Scripture. From this account we learn who bears God's image, that it was God's good idea and what humanity is to do in light of image-bearing.

In the opening chapter of the Book of Genesis, we see a King bring order to His creation. Out of a mysterious, formless creation of His making, He separated light from darkness. Out of a watery heap, He separated waters above from waters below. He adorned the expanse of the heavens with lights that took turns revealing His glory, separating day from night. And at the apex of this creative process He formed man from the dust of the ground and brought from his side the rib He would use to make woman. By Genesis 2, instead of the separation language we hear echoed in the creation of the sky and sea, light and darkness, day and night, new language is heard. We hear the language of "not separate" as the God of creation asserts that "It is not good that man should be alone (same Hebrew stem as *separate, without complement*)..." (Gen. 2:18).

After the creation account in Genesis 1, analogies abound about day and night, light and darkness, and the heavens and the deep (Gen. 8:2; John 9:4; Job 12:22). God graciously seeks to speak the language of a limited people by offering references to things we understand or at least can see. These analogies never speak to the intrinsic value of one over the other. It is not likely that we would ever argue how much better the sky is than the sea or how much better it is that we have days than nights. The truth is we need both. So, it is with humanity. Not only do we need man, we need woman.

So why the struggle? Why does the conversation of a woman's value remain necessary and relevant? Why is there a pervasive wrestle with identity and worth and the seemingly endless pursuit to answer the questions, "What is my value?" and "Am I enough?"

SYMPTOMS FROM THE CULTURE

The message our culture and world communicate concerning the value of women is often in contradiction with Genesis. It is a message focused on outward appearance and accomplishments, and this message favors categories of women such as those with certain achievements, body types, skin tones, with particular views, of a certain age group, marital or socioeconomic status, but it rarely includes all women. These messages are symptoms of not embracing a theologically sound view of what it means to be made in the image of God. In various stages of life, I have encountered such symptoms.

I fondly remember the seven years I spent as a stay-at-home mom. It was a season of great humbling as the credentials that had afforded me upward mobility in the workplace were unimpressive to my new, young employers. Outside the home, sometimes my domestic role was treated as the default for those who lacked skill and options and not always as one worthy of dignity and respect. My husband and I didn't get far into that season of life before recognizing that while my role was traditional, it was not always popular among women who had chosen to make a career outside of the home. Conversely in corporate settings, my value to the company was inextricably tied to my work product and my ability to earn wealth. The message of the corporate world was loud and clear: performance equals value.

Refusing to be localized to work and school, these cultural symptoms also showed up in the community. Ballet performances quickly brought my children into contact with standards on what is considered traditionally beautiful. My daughters' dark, coily hair's resistance to neatly fitting into the traditional ballerina's tidy little bun, quickly ushered us into conversations about what real beauty is and how that shapes the way we are to think about a woman's value.

Amidst a barrage of conflicting messages, how then do we embrace a healthy view of a woman's value? Cultural norms quickly fail us in the conversation and position us to see only a narrow part of the story while dismissing the full scope of redemptive history. Starting in the middle of the narrative informs the conversation on how women are valued but speaks little to the actual value of women. If we are to think rightly about the value of women, we must necessarily start at the beginning.

COMMUNION WITH GOD

In Genesis 1:26, God [*Elohim*] in deliberation with the Son and the Spirit[1] says, "Let us make man (or mankind) in our image, after our likeness." What is immediately obvious from the "us" language, is that creating mankind was to be a collaborative effort. Mankind was to reflect a community that was already in existence in the Godhead, having members

equal in dignity and value yet beautifully diverse in function
(Phil. 2:5-7). Jesus refers to this community as He prays to the
Father in the High Priestly Prayer of John 17. In verse 5, He
asks that the Father return Him to the glory that He enjoyed
in the Father's presence before the world began. He reveals
the interpersonal nature of the persons of the Trinity and
their mutual giving of honor to one another. It is out of the
beauty of this union we hear the words, "Let us make man in
our image."

To create mankind was to invite them into this
community. In Psalm 8:4, the psalmist expresses the sheer
wonder of this lofty notion saying, "What is man that you are
mindful of him and the son of man that you care for him?"
He continues to ponder humanity's value to the Creator in
verse 5 saying, "Yet you have made him a little lower than God
[*Elohim*]" (NASB). Not only do the persons of the Trinity enjoy
a mutual honor, but in making mankind in the image of God
invited humanity into that dignity and honor.

While it is clear that both male and female were made in
the image of God, it is also clear that there are distinctions in
how they were created. Man was created from the dust of the
ground (Gen. 2:7) while woman was formed from the man's rib
(Gen. 2:21). Like man, image-bearing for the woman finds its
first expression in communion with God. Before she is ever
brought to man in 2:22, woman is in the presence of her Father
being formed by Him. Being made in His image, she is the
object of His delight and designed to worship and commune
with her Father.

IMAGE AND LIKENESS

So, what exactly does it mean that she is made "in [His]
image" and "after [His] likeness"? Image *(tselem)* is generally
used to refer to a solid representation of something, while
likeness *(demut)* is a more general term for resemblance.
Because there is no "and" joining the two phrases and because
of their interchangeable usage in subsequent passages, i.e.,
Genesis 1:27 "in God's image" and Genesis 5:1 "in the likeness
of God," it is reasonable to conclude that the two phrases refer
to the same thing, with each clarifying the other.[2]

The "image" terminology would have required no further clarification for the original hearers. In ancient Near Eastern culture, placing an image [*tselem*] or an idol [also *tselem*] of the king in his kingdom was a way that the king declared dominion over his empire. The story of the creation of man followed a familiar narrative. Upon the completion of the creation of His earthly kingdom, God places an image of Himself in His kingdom to express His reign and sovereign rule.[3] This image is first expressed through Adam and Eve. God's placement of both Adam and Eve in the Garden suggests that image-bearing is not about autonomy but about being in communion with the Sovereign[4] and, subsequently, in communion will all others who are in communion with Him.

COMMUNION WITH MAN

When Eve is first brought to Adam, he waxes poetic:

> *"This at last is bone of my bones*
> *and flesh of my flesh;*
> *she shall be called Woman,*
> *because she was taken out of Man"* (Gen. 2:23).

To suggest that this was merely an outflow of Adam's sexual attraction to Eve is to make little of man and less of woman. More than that, Adam only knows his maleness in the presence of Eve's femaleness. Man and woman are wholly themselves in the context of relationship. Eve was someone with whom Adam could enjoy God and engage in the shared work of exercising dominion over the earth. More than just sexual attraction, Adam and Eve were given the gift of being known by someone who was their complement. They were given someone who shared their delight and union with God. Adam and Eve had been given the gift of community with one another by first being invited into community with God. Image-bearing necessarily preceded their communion with God. Their communion with God preceded their community with one another, and their community with one another preceded their mission.

HUMANITY ON MISSION

Immediately following the declaration that man and woman are made in the image of God, Genesis 1:28 names the joint work that mankind is given to do. God invites man and woman into vice-regency with Him by telling them to have dominion over every living thing that moves upon the earth. He gives humanity the joint work of being fruitful and multiplying, as He had also instructed the sea life and land animals in 1:22. He further dignifies humanity in their vice-regency with the noble tasks of filling and subduing the earth and having dominion over it.

At first blush, this may seem like a change of topic in Scripture, but far from it. This work, also known as the Cultural Mandate, is the mission that is central to what it means to be human. Image-bearing is more than the cute family resemblance of a child to her Father. Image-bearing is about a people set on mission to reflect the character of a King throughout His kingdom. At its core, image-bearing demands culture-building, and culture-building involves character-spreading. The work of building culture was a mandate to express the mutual dignity and beautiful diversity found in the community of the Godhead. This work of subduing and filling the earth was not a work given only to Adam and Eve but is necessarily generational. "Filling the earth requires both multiplication and time."[5]

THE EFFECTS OF THE FALL

The rebellion of our first parents did not cause the mandate to be rescinded. Instead, Scripture reveals that this directive has been upheld and renewed. Genesis 9:6 upholds the image of God in man even in humanity's fallen state saying, "Whoever sheds the blood of man, by man shall his blood be shed, for God made man in his own image." Not only does this statement demonstrate that the image of God was not destroyed by the original sin of our first parents, it also reminds the hearers that image-bearing means mission. The verse subsequent to the declaration of image-bearing (just as in Gen. 1:27-28) tells of what the people are to do as a result of being made in the image of God. They are to be on mission, being fruitful, multiplying, and filling the earth. This is not new language but the language of a covenant being renewed, a King's mandate being reiterated, and the image of God being affirmed in fallen humanity.

Understanding this truth, that the image of God remains in all of humanity, informs how we are to ascribe value to all people, not just to those associated with the church. Image-bearing is the essence of what it means to be human and includes every imaginable subset and grouping of people. To ascribe lesser or greater value to any one group is to deny the equality, dignity and diversity of the persons of the Trinity and the honor that all of humanity has been invited into through image-bearing.

CHRIST IS THE IMAGE OF GOD

Although the image of God remains in the whole of humanity, the pervasive effects of the fall of man includes the marring of the image of God in all of humanity. This marring, however, did not rescind God's purposes or direction for the work He had given mankind. It just made the work more difficult to perform (Gen. 3:16-19).[6] In His great mercy, before ever announcing the newfound difficulty of the work, in Genesis 3:15, God proclaims the good news of One who would provide a lasting remedy for the sin that marred His image in mankind. The model and norm for the restoration of the *Imago Dei* is Jesus Christ who is the express image of God (Heb. 1:3).[7] The restoration then of God's image in humanity is only gained through union with Christ and can never be gained apart from Him. In the same way that Adam and Eve's communion with God brought them into community with each other, so it is when we are united with Christ. This union inextricably joins all who believe on the Lord Jesus Christ to one another and brings them into a shared community and mission.

IMAGE-BEARING IN MINISTRY

Peter's understanding of this truth is on display in Acts 9. In a culture that didn't necessarily value women, Peter raised Dorcas from the dead. Dorcas, being full of good works and charity, is first described as a disciple—a follower of Jesus. Dorcas had a vibrant ministry to the widows that was evidenced in how they responded to her death. When Peter arrived at the upper room where Dorcas' body lay, the widows stood weeping, showing Peter tunics and garments Dorcas had made them. She had been an encouragement to the widows in her care for them. There is no mention of a husband for Dorcas. She is possibly widowed or single. While the widows are known by who is absent from their lives, Dorcas is known by Who is present in hers. Her identity is so associated with Christ that it's how she is introduced. This follower of Jesus played a major role in the life and service of the church. When she died, the disciples sent for Peter in a town twelve miles away asking him to perform a miracle of which there is no record he had previously performed. Perhaps their seeming desperation speaks to their great compassion for Dorcas, but quite possibly it also speaks to the value her ministry had in the life of the church.

This one, identified with Christ, served those who would have been on the lowest rungs of the social ladder. She ministered to those who were without power, easily overlooked and forgotten. She invited these marginalized image-bearers into dignity and honor. There's no who's who in her ministry to these women. Instead, the name that is preeminent is that of the One being followed—Jesus.

As a follower of Jesus, Dorcas valued what God valued, those made in His image. Like Jesus, she invited the marginalized back into their God-given dignity. Jesus' ministry was characterized by valuing the lowly. He called the woman with a bleeding issue out of the isolating oppression of her sickness into identity with Him with just one word, daughter (Mark 5:34). He transferred the woman at the well from a life of promiscuity into a new life flowing with living water (John 4:17-18, 10, 13-14). He was pleased to count Mary worthy of learning at His feet when she was being pressured to take on a more traditional role of service (Luke 10:41-42). He embraced all people as worthy of dignity and rejected every system of exclusion. Christ's example nullifies ageism, sexism, racism, classism, tribalism and every other system of inequity that is a revaluation of human worth and a rejection of the image of God He perfectly embodies.

HOW THEN SHALL WE LIVE?

In order to more fully understand the image of God, not only should we look back at creation and at the current implications of redemption, but we must also look at the final destiny of those who are in Christ. Those in union with Christ have been freed from being slaves to sin and, by the Spirit's enabling power, are able to not sin (Rom. 6:22). In the life to come the image of God will be perfected once again in those who are in union with Him. After the resurrection of these mortal bodies, those in Christ will no longer be able to sin or die as they will be raised incorruptible and immortal (1 Cor. 15:53).

The apostle John describes the beauty of this diverse multitude of image-bearers from every nation, from all tribes and peoples and languages, men and women, standing before the throne and before the Lamb, all clothed in white robes, with palm branches in their hands (Rev. 7:9) now assembled for the joint work of worshiping creation's King forever. John also reminds us what it means to have the image restored in humanity saying, "Beloved, we are God's children now, and what we will be has not yet appeared; but we know that when he appears we shall be like him, because we shall see him as he is" (1 John 3:2).

"Because not one word of God's creational design and intent has ever been annulled, the Garden call heard by our first parents still holds and still tells us who and what we are."[8] Culture can never fully suffice in showing a woman her value. She discovers her value in her resemblance to the Creator: when she sets her gaze on the Father, knowing His delight; when she is in union with the Son, growing in His likeness daily; and when she is empowered by the Spirit for a joint mission, spreading His character into all of life. May we see with increasing clarity the One who has invited us to bear His image and may we know our true value in Him.

Vanessa K. Hawkins is the Director of Women's Ministry at First Presbyterian Church in Augusta, GA and holds a Master of Divinity from Covenant Theological Seminary.

DISCUSSION QUESTIONS

1. What do you understand God's purposes in our image-bearing to be?

2. How has image-bearing been marred? How is it being redeemed?

3. In what ways are women (including teens) in your church influenced by cultural, rather than biblical, teachings about the value of women?

4. In what ways does your current context reflect a joint mission for flourishing? In what ways would you like to see it improve?

5. How are you teaching the doctrine of Imago Dei in your women's ministry?

1   C. John Collins, *Genesis 1-4 – A Linguistic, Literary, and Theological Commentary* (Phillipsburg, NJ: P & R Publishing, 2006), 61.
2   Ibid., 62.
3   Gerhard von Rad, *Genesis: A Commentary* (Louisville: Westminster John Knox Press, 1973), 59-60.
4   J. Todd Billings, *Union with Christ: Reframing Theology and Ministry for the Church* (Grand Rapids, MI: Baker Academic, 2011), 33.
5   Michael D. Williams, "God and Humanity: The Human as *Imago Dei*," (Covenant Theological Seminary, Spring 2018), 148.
6   Ibid., 145.
7   Ibid., 153.
8   Ibid., 145.

Chapter 5

Unity in the Body of Christ:
A Study of Ephesians 4:1-16
Catherine Chang

"The fact remains that the church of God, far from being a
tangled heap of wreckage, is even now God's own perfectly
proportioned temple, built upon the foundation of the
apostles and prophets, with Jesus Christ Himself as the chief
cornerstone, in whom all the building is fitly framed together
and all believers are built together for a habitation of God
through the Spirit . . . God omniscient sees it thus. So does
God's child with the eye of faith."[1] —R.B. Kuiper

Division. Church splits. Gossip. Discontent. Bitterness.
Jealousy. If you have ever been deeply invested in the
life of the church, I bet that you have been witness
to these things and more. As Christians all know, we *ought*
to have unity, so that by our love for one another, the world
will know and praise our Father in heaven. Yet in reality,
this is often not the case. Perhaps you are in a church that
is currently experiencing a wonderful season of joyful unity
among its members, and if this is so, I join you in praising God
for that! However, for many of us, there is a deep sense that
something is not quite right in our struggle as believers to
maintain the unity by the power of the Holy Spirit.

Ephesians 4:1-16 is considered by many to be one of the
classic passages on the topic of unity in the church, and as
such, much has already been written on this particular text.
Why review it here? As we seek to grow as leaders who are
actively involved in the life of the church, it is imperative
that we have a biblical understanding of exactly what we
are striving to cultivate in our churches. As *women* leaders,

we have likely been witness to the destruction that can be wrought when sisters are not committed to unity, and we have also experienced the blessings of grace, forgiveness, and growth when sisters *are* committed to unity. In her book, *The True Woman*, Susan Hunt points out that the helper role we were created to fill is one that is characterized by a call to community and compassion.[2] As such, we have been wonderfully designed with a special capacity to encourage unity in the body. However, when we lose sight of this special call, we can equally be the source of much discord. This chapter then, shows us the biblical understanding of true unity since we, as leaders, have a special opportunity and responsibility to promote in our women's ministries the type of unity and community Scripture sets forth for us, a unity that is centered on the gospel and that is deeply inclusive of all types of women in all walks of life. This text affords us a wonderful look at the doctrine and practice of unity in the body of Christ.

THE CALL TO WALK IN A WORTHY MANNER IS A CALL TO UNITY

Chapter 4 of Ephesians opens with the apostle Paul's introduction, "I therefore." As many of us have learned in our study of the Scriptures, when we see a "therefore," we have to ask why it is there. Scholars agree that this transition from chapters 1-3 to chapters 4-6 represents a transition in Paul's thinking from doctrine to practice, from the description of grace to the implications of grace,[3] from the theological indicative to the ethical imperative. In other words, having understood the glorious nature of what God has done for us in Christ as enumerated in the first three chapters, now we are able to see what that means for us as we live in light of our identity as His chosen and redeemed people.

The command to walk in a manner worthy of the calling to which we have been called requires that we understand the glorious redemption from which that calling arises. What the Bible says about the relationship between redemption and action, salvation and work, is at the core of this conversation about unity. Many Christians, myself included, still have a lingering misconstrued notion of how our faith lived out relates to how our God sees us. Yes, we know that it is by grace we have been saved not of ourselves (Eph. 2:8)—yet at times we can struggle with a subtle feeling that at some level, what we do impacts how much God loves us or wants to bless us. What Paul emphasizes here is that this call to walk as God would have us walk is based entirely on the fact that there is no way we could ever do this of our own strength, ability, or desire! This imperative comes after three chapters of driving home the truth of the gospel that it is God in Christ who has done the work. It is only in full realization of and dependence upon this fact that we can now enter into chapter 4 where Paul greets us by telling us that our task as God's chosen people is to live up to the glory of salvation in Christ. Until we truly realize that our redemption has already been accomplished in Christ by grace, all our striving will be futile and can lead only to frustration and disappointment. However, when we, in light of Paul's teaching, are able to say, "*Therefore* because I am who I am by grace, I will walk by grace," we can continue on to unearth the riches of what this calling entails.

What then does it look like to walk in a manner worthy of the calling? Verse 2 describes for us a life that is characterized by humility and gentleness, patience, and forbearance. It is valuable to note here that these were not qualities that were prized at the time of Paul's writing. Rather, humility or lowliness of mind,[4] and gentleness or meekness[5] were seen as signs of weakness in the ancient world. Paul here rejects the cultural and societal norms in favor of a kingdom vision. That vision is significant for us in that all the characteristics listed here point to one goal, which is the maintaining of the unity of the Spirit. When Paul describes the life worthy of the calling, it is a life lived unto unity. We have not only been called out of darkness into light, we have been called out of death and into the life of a community with other believers. Whether our present circumstances seem so or not, whether we feel it or not, we are part of this glorious body of Christ! This reality should shake us out of complacency and give us a renewed sense of urgency in how we participate in the life of the body.

THE BASIS OF OUR UNITY

When we look at the state of many churches today, we certainly do not feel assured of the fact of this unity. We see brokenness and division on many fronts that would seem to more definitively indicate an underlying *dis*unity. So how can we claim unity in the midst of seemingly contradictory circumstances? Verse 3 points out that this is a unity in the Holy Spirit. It is a God-initiated and sustained unity that is grounded in the triune nature of God Himself. It is a unity that is not manmade and so cannot be destroyed by man, no matter how hard we try!

Verses 4 through 6 then give us wonderful insight into the nature of the unity we have in the body. Within these three verses, there are seven "one" statements that serve as beautiful reflections of a communal, relational, and unified God. Commentators differ as to how we ought to understand these statements in relation to one another, but I appreciate one commentator who points out that Paul's statements here have a trinitarian and theological structure: 1) body, Spirit, hope (v. 4); 2) Lord, faith, baptism (v. 5); 3) one God and Father of all, who is over all, through all, and in all (v. 6).[6] We see in this simplified breakdown that Paul is emphasizing for us how our triune God calls us who are many to live as one in light of the one gospel we profess.

If we further examine these verses, we find confirmation that the call to unity is not a feel-good, superficial unity that would ignore our differences. On the contrary, it is a unity that demands that we hold firmly to the deep theological truths of the gospel. Our unity in the body must never come at the expense of truth.[7] Paul makes sure of this by using the language of verse 4 to hearken back to verse 1, reminding us that a called and worthy life is first grounded in the person and work of Christ, and is a life lived with unity in view. The Spirit-unified body is the image of the heavenly hope we hold onto.[8]

Verse 5 then points us to the second person of the Trinity, the Lord Jesus, who is the substance of our faith, as well as the object of our baptism since all believers are united in Him.[9] The trinitarian call to unity concludes by summing up all things in the God and Father of all who is over all, through all, and in all, and, therefore, the basis of our unity. Our unity is founded and built upon the very nature of the God we profess. It is a God-initiated and indestructible oneness.

DIVERSITY IN UNITY

What should this unity look like? Recently, I was looking at old college photos and came across several from the campus fellowship I had belonged to. One thing that struck me as I flipped through the photos was how we were dressed. The women in particular all wore similar dresses. These were dresses that "good" Christian college girls wore for group photos: flowery, modest, floor-length dresses. While there are certainly worse things than wearing unflattering frocks, the underlying belief was that unity meant uniformity and sameness. In the Scripture, Paul shows us that unity in the body, in fact, means something completely different.

Verse 7 marks a notable turn from the previous verse. After speaking about the God and Father of *all*, Paul turns swiftly, "*but* grace was given to *each one* of us." He moves from a strong urge toward unity to a strong reminder that that unity comes through individuals in the body. We are not called to homogeneity; rather, we are called to embrace the grace that has been given to each one of us by Christ Himself, our triumphant and generous King (cf. Ps. 68:18). It is important to note that the grace mentioned here is not salvation grace, but a service grace[10] or grace for ministry[11] and is generally understood to refer to the gifts enumerated in verse 11.

The list of gifts in this passage is different from other lists in the New Testament, and none of them are identical or exhaustive. There are five categories listed here: apostles, prophets, evangelists, shepherds, and teachers. All the gifts listed by Paul are clearly pointed toward the leadership of the church and focus again on the importance of upholding the truth of Scripture as they are primarily Word-based gifts. Does this then indicate that only the leaders of the church are gifted to serve the body? No. The beauty of this passage is that it is a primary text for the support of every member being involved in ministry in the church. In verse 12, we see that these particular gifts are listed because they are the means for the leadership to equip God's people for the work of ministry and to build up the body of Christ.

This should serve as both an encouragement and a rebuke for those of us in the church who are not in official positions of service. Why? What Paul explicitly states in this passage is that these gifts are given to equip all the saints for works of ministry. All the saints. What an amazing encouragement it is for us that our sovereign God desires that each one of us should be equipped to do His work! For those of us who have long been taught that it is only the pastor or the ordained men of the church who should do most of the church's ministry, Paul says, "No!" Ministry is given to every believer in Christ, and it is Christ Himself who gifts and empowers us to accomplish the tasks to which we are called.[12] Naturally, the exact form of these ministry tasks will vary from person to person, under the wisdom and rule of the church's leadership.

This idea of "every-member" ministry[13] should also gently rebuke those of us who have been church members for years, perhaps even most of our lives, and yet feel no sense of responsibility for the work of ministry. It is clear from Scripture that a life that lives out the calling of God should work toward the goal of unity, and this certainly entails being an active and vital part of the church body.

LIVING OUT OUR UNITY

What then is the purpose of these gifts and the building up of the body (v. 12)? Paul tells us in verse 13 that we are to build up the body until we all attain to the unity of the faith and to mature manhood to the measure of the stature of the fullness of Christ. There is a two-fold end in view here: first to attain unity, and second to attain maturity.

However, did we not spend the first several verses of this chapter ensuring that we understand that we already have this unity in Christ through the Spirit? Why would Paul implore us to attain something we already have? What we see here is a picture of the sum of our reality as redeemed believers sojourning in a still broken world. We are an already redeemed, justified, sanctified, raised-up people, though not yet as we shall be in glory. First Corinthians 13:12 says, "For now we see in a mirror dimly, but then face to face. Now I know in part; then I shall know fully, even as I have been fully known." This tension between the already and the not-yet is depicted here in Paul's discussion of unity in the body. We have already been made one in the body through our invisible union with Christ, yet we are also to strive to maintain this invisible reality visible in the church[14] and to attain to the fullness of it, though imperfectly this side of heaven.

Secondly, part of our goal is to attain maturity, "the measure of the stature of the fullness of Christ" (v. 13). This, too, is a goal we must continually strive toward, though imperfectly in this life. Paul paints for us a picture of the differences between immaturity and maturity by setting up several contrasting images: children vs. mature manhood, tossed to and fro vs. joined and held together, cunning and deceit vs. love and truth.[15] Too often, we in the church find ourselves still acting as children, being tossed around in our biblical understanding, struggling with being rooted in self-centeredness and self-protection rather than growing up into Him who has made us and given us and called us for so much more. So how do we attain maturity?

SPEAKING TRUTH IN LOVE
Verse 15 shows us the way. English translations of this verse do not quite carry the same connotation as the original Greek. The word here, *aletheuontes*, is a verb form of "truth," so if we had such a word, it could be translated "truthing in love." Speaking truth is certainly in view here; however, there is an even greater and more holistic sense of living out the truth in all things.

Truth. When we speak, what exactly are we to say? Herein lies a great challenge for the church: what is the truth we are to speak? We are inundated with "truth" from all sides: a psychologized culture that seeks to label and classify, yet often without addressing deeper issues of the heart, political correctness, personal experience, an entertainment-driven, consumer mindset. These all play into what we believe to be the truth. As Christians, we ought to say the Bible is the source and foundation for all of life, but in practice all these other influences have much more sway over us than perhaps we would like to admit. It is not to say that all culture or experience is devoid of truth, since under common grace we know that we still see God's faithfulness in the world. However, if these worldly lenses become the primary framework through which we define truth, we will find ourselves lacking. First Corinthians 1:20 reminds us of this: "Where is the one who is wise? Where is the scribe? Where is the debater of this age? Has not God made foolish the wisdom of the world?"

We spend our days being pressed in on from all sides by the things our society pushes us to accept as truth, so that when the time comes to speak biblical truth, we often find ourselves at a loss. It is easier to toss out common sense, wisdom aggregated from a multitude of sources, because that is where we live and breathe, but Scripture calls us to do better. How can we pour forth a wisdom that we ourselves have not known? To speak from a biblical worldview requires a deep personal commitment to learning and studying true wisdom. Where do we find this wisdom? We find it in a Person (1 Cor. 1:30-31). It is in knowing Christ, who is our wisdom, that we can become wise. It is in studying the Word and seeing the breadth and depth of the wisdom of an all-knowing God, that we are able to speak truth—His truth. Throughout this Ephesians passage, Paul hammers home how imperative it is that we be grounded in Scripture. As we consider love, we must note that biblical love cannot exist apart from biblical truth.

Love. The love in which we are to speak is not the kind of love depicted in Hollywood movies. It is the love of a gracious God to wretched sinners, demonstrated in the sacrifice of Christ on the cross. It is a love that, when rightly understood, pierces us and transforms us. It is a love that will not let sin go unaddressed. It is a love that weeps in others' suffering and rejoices in their triumphs. It is a love that says the hard things, but also at times says nothing at all and simply holds a friend close. We need to know this love and be firmly rooted in it in our hearts, for it is out of the overflow of the heart that our mouths speak. Left to ourselves, when we look at the brokenness and sinfulness in the world, in the people around us, and in our own lives, it is impossible to speak truth in love. However, when we know the Savior and the grace and love we have received, we can love because He first loved us.

CONCLUSION

How do we attain to this maturity in Christ? We speak truth in love. We know, study, and cherish the truth of the gospel, and we love as those who have ourselves been sacrificially and unconditionally loved by God. As we do this, we find that speaking truth in love is both the means of our communal growth *and* the fruit of it. As women, I believe that God has created us with a great ability to know and speak into the lives of others. Apart from dependence on His grace, this ability can become twisted, manipulative, and destructive, but, as we grow in grace, we find that we can be used increasingly as instruments of redemption as we use our words to build up the body.

My prayer for women's ministry leaders and for all the women in our churches is that we would take seriously the command to walk in a manner worthy of the calling we have received. We need to be reminded of our calling to live in light of all that God has done in Christ. This is a calling to live in unity as vital members of the body of Christ, a calling to attain to maturity and the fullness of Him who called us.

Catherine Chang received her MDiv in biblical counseling from Westminster Seminary in Philadelphia. She and her family reside in Southern California where she serves as the children's ministry director at her church.

DISCUSSION QUESTIONS

1. We have been called to live a life in unity. How deep is the sense of this calling in your life?

2. Which aspects of biblical unity are new to you or resonate with you?

3. How does the concept of "every-member ministry" encourage or challenge you?

4. What are some areas in which your ministry can grow in unity? Where have you experienced challenges? How does the biblical understanding of unity meet you in those challenges?

5. In which specific ways can you grow in speaking truth in love?

1   R.B. Kuiper, *The Glorious Body of Christ* (London: Wm B. Eerdmans, 1966), 43.
2   Susan Hunt, *The True Woman* (Wheaton, IL: Crossway Books, 1997), 107.
3   Klyne Snodgrass, *NIV Application Commentary: Ephesians* (Grand Rapids: Zondervan, 1996), 194.
4   John R. W. Stott, *The Bible Speaks Today: The Message of Ephesians* (Downers Grove, Inter-Varsity Press, 1979), 148.
5   Ibid., 149.
6   Snodgrass, *Ephesians*, 198.
7   Kevin DeYoung, "Toward a Theology of Church Unity," DeYoung, Restless, and Reformed, The Gospel Coalition, October 9, 2012, www.thegospelcoalition.org/blogs/kevin-deyoung/toward-a-theology-of-church-unity/.
8   Peter T. O'Brien, *The Pillar New Testament Commentary: The Letter to the Ephesians* (Grand Rapids: William B. Eerdmans, 1999), 280.
9   Ibid., 284.
10 Stott, *Message of Ephesians*, 155.
11 Snodgrass, *Ephesians*, 200.
12 R. Kent Hughes, *Ephesians: The Mystery of the Body of Christ* (Wheaton: Crossway, 1990), 130.
13 Stott, *Message of Ephesians*, 167.
14 Ibid., 169.
15 Snodgrass, *Ephesians*, 206.

Chapter 6

The Stability of the Word in a Shifting World: Theological Essentials for a Philosophy of Women's Ministry

Paula Miles and Teri Anderson

Where were you on 9/11 when the World Trade Center's Twin Towers came down? Every generation has a unifying event, and we mark change from that point forward. Since 9/11/2001, cultural change has accelerated. We've had shifts in travel security, how we make phone calls, and in architectural safety. We have experienced political polarization, seen the creation of social media, and witnessed gender identity confusion. Experiencing these changes makes us wonder: Does Women's Ministry need to recalibrate in order to be relevant in our culture? Is our current philosophy of ministry outdated? As reflected in the issues addressed in this book, women are trying to determine what it looks like to live in the changing culture and address contemporary issues with biblical answers.

Whether it was the fall of Jerusalem in 70 AD, Christians fleeing Europe to settle America in the 1600s, or the fight for Civil Rights for African-Americans in 1960s America, a changing world has always existed for believers. Although nothing seems certain or truly lasting, One exists, who is constant, sure, and lasting. God does not change (James 1:17). His plan cannot be thwarted (Isa. 14:24). His Word transcends time. "The grass withers, the flower fades, but the word of our God will stand forever" (Isa. 40:8).

God reveals His Truth to us by the work of the Holy Spirit through Scripture. This Word is breathed out by Him and is useful in our lives to equip and to make us complete (2 Tim.

3:16-17). Because the Bible is God-breathed, it brings life and teaches how to live in His kingdom (Deut. 32:47). We learn that the Word not only gives life but is actually alive (Heb. 4:12; 1 Peter 1:23; Acts 7:38). God by His Word brings us to a saving knowledge of Himself (1 Peter 1:23), then continues to work in us, transforming us into the image of His Son (1 Thess. 2:13). Just like physical food, we need God's Word to nourish and sustain us spiritually, and to instruct us how to function as God's people (Matt. 4:4).

The Word of God is the foundation for a biblical worldview. Everyone has a worldview. Someone or something is informing our views. We are conformed to the world's worldview if we are not transformed by Scripture. Some women conform to the secular world. Others conform to practices that look "religious," but result in rules-based "checklist" living. Yet others retreat to an insulated, Christian subculture. However, God calls us to real, lasting transformation. God calls believers to renew our minds with the truth of the gospel daily and to learn to view the world through His eyes (2 Cor. 5:1). Romans 12:2 provides a guide for Christians, "Do not be conformed to this world, but be transformed by the renewal of your mind, that by testing you may discern what is the will of God, what is good and acceptable and perfect." As the Holy Spirit works in our lives and changes us, we begin to see the world from a biblical perspective. We begin to understand that God has saved us unto Himself, to honor and glorify Him: "and he died for all, that those who live might no longer live for themselves but for him who for their sake died and was raised" (2 Cor. 5:15). Scripture teaches that all God's creation is His kingdom. "The LORD has established his throne in the heavens, and his kingdom rules over all" (Ps. 103:19). The boundary between "sacred" and "secular" fades away, since He created it all, and it belongs to Him. Scripture teaches that every aspect of our lives should reflect the glory of God, "So, whether you eat or drink, or whatever you do, do all to the glory of God" (1 Cor. 10:31). We go grocery shopping and cook meals, create a sculpture, compete in sports, are godly employees or supervisors—all to the glory of God.

A BIBLICAL PHILOSOPHY FOR WOMEN'S MINISTRY

A philosophy for women's ministry should embody three components of biblically sound discipleship. First, our ministry must be Word-based. Scripture must be the foundation of our ministry framework, and our discipleship approach needs to involve an intentional decision to make consistent application of God's Word to our ministry. In Romans 12:1, before Paul commands us to be transformed by the renewing of our minds, he urges us in view of the mercy of God "to present your bodies as a living sacrifice, holy and acceptable to God, which is your spiritual [logical] worship." As we evaluate our discipleship ministries, we need to ask, "Do they provide opportunities for women to study the Word so they will better understand the mercy of God?"

Do we provide a place where the Spirit can do His transforming work, where women will be equipped to glorify God in all of life? If so, God's kingdom may be extended, and the results of our women's ministry work will be an act of worship to Him. If not, how can we modify our stated motivation for both our formal and our informal ministries?

Second, if we have a Word-based ministry, we need to evaluate if it is a purely academic, knowledge-based-only approach to ministry. Does transforming the mind *alone* conform us to the image of Christ? Many Christians believe knowledge and personal piety *are* the ultimate goals of discipleship. If Bible studies are focused merely upon accumulating knowledge, even content that is biblically informed can lead to in-grown Bible studies that study Scripture for the sake of studying it. In addition, there are a plethora of ways to personally study the Bible by using study guides or commentaries, reading blogs, or listening to sermon podcasts. With so many tools, we may start believing that studying the Bible alone, by ourselves, is the best way to study God's Word. Individual time or small group time spent in the Word should not be abandoned, but ask, what is the outflow of all the Bible study women in our church are doing?

Our ministry to women must recognize that in addition to a focused study of Scripture, a vital relational component exists in God's kingdom. When God saves us, He adopts us into His family.

Ephesians 1:5 says, "He predestined us for adoption to himself as sons through Jesus Christ, according to the purpose of his will." Salvation graces us with both a vertical (to God) and a horizontal component (to others). "So we, though many, are one body in Christ, and individually members of one another" (Rom. 12:5). God creates a kingdom-minded family, identified not only as the worldwide church universal (Heb. 12:22-23), but He also calls us into community as members of a local church. Jesus modeled this relational component Himself with His disciples. Later in Ephesians 4:11-16, the apostle Paul also reminds us that God gives gifts of Word ministry to His people in order "to equip the saints for the work of ministry, for building up the body of Christ, until we all attain to the unity of the faith and of the knowledge of the Son of God, to mature manhood, to the measure of the stature of the fullness of Christ." God never intended for us to live the Christian life on our own, no matter when or where He places us in redemptive history. "Relationships are an irreplaceable tool in God's redemptive hands."[1]

A Word-based, relationally-driven women's ministry model is where truth and love dwell hand-in-hand and enhance transformation. If we only care about knowledge with no concern for gospel relationships, our ministry is academic. If relationships are all that matter and are not undergirded by the truth of God's Word, our ministry is anemic. Finding the balance to have both a Word-based and a relational ministry might mean evaluating your women's ministry programs to see how each small group study incorporates community building or how each fellowship event incorporates teaching time.

Third, in addition to designing a Word-based ministry that occurs in the context of relationships, a solid biblical foundation for women's ministry includes outreach and service. When a discipleship ministry arises out of Scripture-based relationships, then a service-driven outreach is the natural overflow. A women's ministry must intentionally incorporate service and evangelism into its discipleship ministries.

Once we confirm that our discipleship ministries are marked with a gospel focus taught in the context of relationships with an overflow of service and outreach, we need to evaluate ministry motivation. Sometimes we let cultural norms for success creep into our ministries when they become personality-driven, program-driven, or consumer-driven.[2] A personality-driven ministry revolves around its leader who structures the ministry according to her preferences rather than being collaborative with other women on the leadership team. The result of this kind of ministry can include the glory going to a person rather than to God and conflict over personal preferences. Other women are rarely given opportunities to use or develop their spiritual gifts, and little time is spent on discipling and equipping new leaders. Consequently, leadership transfer is difficult, and without a particular leader, the ministry often dies. As a local church women's Bible study teacher, I (Teri) noticed this phenomenon occurring when women were unwilling to step into teaching roles, expressing feelings of inadequacies or inexperience. I started rotating in "guest teachers" monthly. We also avoided popularity contests by intentionally not listing a teacher's name on Bible study sign-ups.

Another way we get side-tracked is to become program- or task-driven. Women are tempted to measure success by the size and quality of events. We forget that the Spirit's transformation of us to become like Christ results in real and lasting fruit that glorifies God. We need to avoid creating a ministry focus where tasks are more important than people and "efficiency trumps community and discipleship."[3] A performance mentality also breeds comparison and territorialism. Before we know it, we forget our ministry purpose and have no idea why we are doing what we are doing.

Finally, we are easily distracted if our women's ministry focuses on consumer-driven society and tries to meet the demands of particular individuals. Like Timothy (2 Tim. 4:1-5), we need to be challenged to teach the Word even when itching ears ask for something else. A consumer-driven, "me-centered" versus a God-centered ministry can present itself in different ways. We want to know the needs of women to whom we are ministering, but we cannot be ruled by their demands. We must prayerfully consider what they really need—a community united around the shared purpose of God's glory.

A ministry centered on God's Word with the focus of God's glory results in the extension of God's kingdom in individual lives, the local church, and beyond. In this setting, transformation is possible, and women are compelled to live for something greater than themselves (2 Cor. 5:15-17). For more than a decade I (Paula) have participated in equipping and training women for ministry throughout the United States as well as internationally. I've witnessed ministries thrive as women commit to teach the content of God's Word in the context of gospel relationships (which outlive any specific person or program) and allow for many different ministry models, regardless of church size.

When women of all races, age groups, and socio-economic backgrounds are grounded in the unchanging truth of Scripture and serve together unified in Christ, the gospel truly does change not only lives but our families, our churches, our communities and ultimately, the world.

Paula Miles serves as the women's ministry coordinator at Clemson Presbyterian Church (PCA).

Teri Anderson has served at Spring Meadows Presbyterian Church (PCA) on the women's ministry team and as a Bible study teacher. Both are trainers for the PCA national women's ministry team.

DISCUSSION QUESTIONS

1. What are some ways you are personally tempted to conform to the world or to Christian subculture?

2. Think of a time when God used His Word by His Spirit to transform your way of thinking. How did your new understanding impact your living?

3. How is God's Word the centerpiece of your life and ministry? How is God's glory your focus? Give examples. Why does it matter?

4. What are ways your women's ministries can avoid being personality-, program-, or consumer-driven in its approach?

5. List practical ways to maintain a healthy tension of context/ truth and content/gospel relationships so that discipleship does not become academic or anemic.

6. How do your discipleship ministries (Bible studies, fellowships, mentoring groups, mercy ministries, etc.) intentionally serve and evangelize in outreach beyond the church community?

7. List any women's ministry focus in your church that needs to be adjusted to display this kingdom discipleship philosophy model. How will this approach help you address contemporary issues with biblical answers?

1   Paul Tripp, *New Morning Mercies* (Wheaton, IL: Crossway, 2014), August 19.
2   PCA Women's Ministry Trainers. *Thinking Biblically and Living Covenantally: A Biblical Apologetic for Women* (Lawrenceville, GA: Committee on Discipleship Ministries, 2014, 2017, 2018, 2019), 70.
3   Karen Hodge and Susan Hunt. *Life-giving Leadership* (Lawrenceville, GA: Committee on Discipleship Ministries, 2018), 169.

Chapter 7

Gospel-Driven Friendship
Melanie Cogdill

Mention the terms *Titus 2 discipleship*, *spiritual mothering*, or *mentoring*, and you can anticipate eye rolling. A key component for the discipleship of women in the local church is for women to be encouraged to develop "Titus 2 friendships." For some, Titus 2 friendships conjures up an image of a group of women standing in a kitchen with aprons on as they make Jell-O salad and talk about rainbows, unicorns, and play dates. "#Lame," they think.

However, women cultivating friendships with other women has become culturally hip. It even has a name: your "squad." Girls on social media like to post memes to their Instagram accounts that have pithy sayings about their squad, such as: "Squad means family, and family means no one gets left behind." Or "When worse comes to worse, squad comes first." The phrase "squad goals" is part of the cultural zeitgeist, probably thanks to pop singer Taylor Swift and her squad of famous friends posting selfies with one another.

If girls or women don't have a squad, how can they find friends? Some women turn to online sources or social media influencers and lifestyle bloggers. Sarah Salvini's YouTube channel has 123,000 subscribers, and in her video "How to Find the Best Friends for You," she says, "As long as you are true to yourself and your opinions, you eliminate the people who aren't really good friends for you or aren't good fits or you don't really want to be around them because they don't fit your needs."[1] The saddest part of this video is the comments section—everyone seems lonely and wants a friend.

But not only young teens or twenty-something girls are

looking for friends. In her *Christianity Today* article "Middle-Aged Women Face a Crisis of Discipleship," author Michelle Van Loon notes, "In local churches, there's often a discipleship gap for older members"(June 8, 2017). It is common for women in midlife to feel ignored by the church. Because of this lack of formal programs for women in midlife, friendships in the church are vital. We are called as God's people (the church) to be in relationship with one another. First Thessalonians 5:14 says, "We urge you, brothers, admonish the idle, encourage the fainthearted, help the weak, be patient with them all."

In the Book of Titus, the apostle Paul addresses the lives of believers both within the church and outside of it. He addresses relationships in the church, and those relationships include women. Titus teaches three things about gospel friendships developed in the context of the entire church.

1. Discipleship relationships are true gospel friendships in the context of the church body. Years ago, when I first heard about Titus 2 mentors, my idea of a Titus 2 friendship was being matched with an older woman at church who would proceed to give me her opinions about how to live my life. That is a misguided understanding of friendships between women in the church.

Friendships between women in the church last for eternity because they are in the context of the body of Christ. They are not independent friend squads of BFFs (Best Friends Forever) who are disconnected from the church body.

In Titus 2, Paul addresses the entire church and, starting in verse 2, urges older men, younger men, older women, and younger women to be sober-minded, dignified, self-controlled, sound in faith, in love and steadfastness. Women likewise are to be self-controlled, pure, kind (v. 7)—a model of good works.

Here are characteristics of gospel-centered relationship that are lived out in the context of the body of Christ, including relationships among women in the church:

- Gospel-driven friendships are safe and characterized by grace (1 Peter 5:5).
- Gospel-driven friendships point one other to God (Eph. 1:6).

- Gospel-driven friendships do not allow excuses to justify sin, and Christians friends are willing to deal with the messiness of life. (*Love* in 1 Cor. 13:6 means not rejoicing in wrongdoing but in truth.)
- Gospel-driven friendships are characterized by the fruit of the Holy Spirit, such as kindness, forgiveness, thanksgiving to God, and love (Col. 3:12-17).
- Gospel-driven friendships believe the best of others (1 Cor. 13:7).
- Gospel-driven friendships sacrifice personal preferences for God's glory and the good of others in the church (Phil. 2:3-5).
- Gospel-driven friendships promote peacemaking (James 3:16-18).
- Gospel-driven friendships are accepting of others (Rom. 15:7) and promote unity (not uniformity or sameness).
- Gospel-driven friendships regularly point one another to the gospel (Titus 3:4).[2]

If your ministry encourages gospel friendships among women in your church, it means no woman should be lonely or isolated—not even women who are on the fringes of church life. Social media has facilitated our ability to avoid people we don't prefer (we can defriend them on Facebook or mute their posts). Social media makes it possible to connect with people who are exactly like us. We can join Facebook groups of very narrow tribes of people with similar interests, such as a group for working moms of teenagers who love cooking, blogging, playing tennis, and scrapbooking twice a month.

Titus 2 friendships are the opposite of social-media friend tribes. All the women in your church should be known and cared for because we are united to Christ as His children. Jesus has called us into relationships with one another.

2. Titus 2 friendships are characterized by theological truth.
Our friendships are not based upon socializing but by true fellowship around the Word in worship and study, in prayer, and serving in ministry together (Acts 2). Titus 1:1 states that the apostle Paul wrote this letter "for the sake of the faith of God's elect and their knowledge of the truth." Titus 2:1 starts

the chapter with an emphasis on teaching sound doctrine. Friendships in the church body (women with other women, men with other men) are to be characterized by biblical truth.

Paul reminds Titus of that in Titus 2:11—that the various discipleship relationships in the church are because of the gospel, "For the grace of God has appeared, bringing salvation for all people." Verse 11 goes on to say that the gospel trains Christians to renounce ungodliness and to live godly lives.

In Titus 3:5-7, Paul reminds Titus once again of his gospel-focused motivation built on doctrinal truth:

But when the goodness and loving kindness of God our Savior appeared, he saved us, not because of works done by us in righteousness, but according to his own mercy, by the washing of regeneration and renewal of the Holy Spirit, whom he poured out on us richly through Jesus Christ our Savior, so that being justified by his grace we might become heirs according to the hope of eternal life.

Our relationships are not exemplified by squad goals. These relationships reflect the very doctrine of God. In Titus 2:10, the friendships of women are a tangible testimony that is stated in Titus 2:5 that the Word of God may not be reviled (which means criticized—so that no one can criticize the Word of God). Verse 10 states that these friendships adorn the doctrine of God. Our relationships make the gospel even more beautiful because they are characterized by biblical truth. Our relationships with other women are not self-serving, self-focused, characterized by gossip, or insulated as BFFs. They are relationships in which the glory of God is reflected.

3. Titus 2 friendships result in the pursuit of godliness.
This is godliness that flows out of a Christ-centered life. In Hendriksen and Kistemaker's commentary on Titus, they write, "The book of Titus stresses the idea that sound doctrine goes hand-in-hand with the life of sanctification."[3] Discipleship relationships point one another to the gospel that trains us to live godly lives right now. Titus 2:11-12 reminds us: "For the grace of God has appeared, bringing salvation for all people,

training us to renounce ungodliness and worldly passions, and to live self-controlled, upright, and godly lives in the present age." Godly women are zealous for good works (Titus 2:14), since it is the gospel that motivates them and drives them to serve God.

Titus 3 describes a life in pursuit of godliness. Christians are ready for every good work (Titus 3:1) and are devoted to good works (Titus 3:8, 14).

The motivation for encouraging one another to live a life of godliness is the gospel, which Paul reminds the church of in Titus 3:4-7:

But when the goodness and lovingkindness of God our Savior appeared, he saved us, not because of works done by us in righteousness, but according to his own mercy, by the washing of regeneration and renewal of the Holy Spirit, whom he poured out on us richly through Jesus Christ our Savior, so that being justified by his grace we might become heirs according to the hope of eternal life.

A SMALL-GROUP MODEL FOR TITUS 2 DISCIPLESHIP
One of the most effective ways a women's ministry can facilitate multigenerational Titus 2 friendships is through a small-group model.[4] Jesus discipled others by using a small-group model. The dynamics of a small group of women allows participants to hear from more than one voice. A multitude of women of various ages, backgrounds, ethnicities, and stages of life allows for the diversity among the body of Christ and assists each woman to grow in her love for God and her love for others. And through a small-group model, one-to-one friendships naturally form as God providentially places women into these groups by bringing women together who might not have known one another otherwise. Our culture should be able to recognize Christian women as being united in Christ. Women are notorious for forming cliques and only wanting to be friends with women who are similar to themselves. Women at times are known for icing out women they don't like, who annoy them, or who don't measure up to a social standard of beauty or socio-economic standing. In the

Gospel of John, in His high priestly prayer, Jesus prays that Christians should have Holy Spirit-driven friendships. We are not of the world. We are different. We welcome all women, no matter how "difficult" a woman seems to us. We not only welcome them but enter into true friendships with them as sisters for all eternity, united in Christ (John 17:20-23).

YOU'VE GOT A FRIEND

It's been said anecdotally that in order to find a friend, one has to be willing to be one. Christian friendships should be different than friendship goals promoted by YouTube and social media influencers. How is that even possible? Women can be cold and cruel, and female friendships can have all kinds of relational challenges caused by circumstances, brokenness, and sin. We cannot be a friend to others apart from the gospel. Our hope is in Christ who is the ultimate friend. He laid down His life not for friends but for enemies and those who hated Him (Rom. 5:6-8). Our prayer for our churches is for them to be places where all women are loved, accepted, and welcomed into the life of the church because Christ Himself is the ultimate friend to us. He bears our burdens. He gives us loving correction. He teaches us from His Word. And He loves us. And those are true marks of real friendship.

Melanie Cogdill is a women's ministry trainer for the Presbyterian Church in America, the managing editor of the CHRISTIAN RESEARCH JOURNAL (equip.org), and host of the weekly podcast *Postmodern Realities* (available on iTunes).

DISCUSSION QUESTIONS

1. Think about sisters in Christ who are good friends at your church. Give specific examples of some of the gospel-driven characteristics that are true of your friendships.

2. How are you developing relationships with godly older women who are further in life's journey from you? How are you proactively initiating being a gospel friend to women who are younger than you?

3. What gospel-centered characteristic would you need prayer for in order to grow as a friend?

4. What are ways in which doctrinal truth characterizes your Christian friendships?

5. How do you reach out to women on the fringes of your church or women who seem "difficult" to you and forge a friendship with them?

6. What are the specific events or programs or small-group ministries in your women's ministry that proactively encourage Titus 2 friendships?

7. Make a list of practical ways Christ is a friend to you.

---

1   Sarah Salvini, "How to Find the Best Friends for You! TRUE FRIENDS," YouTube video, 4:23. Posted March 9, 2016, https://www.youtube.com/watch?v=C1WMWuuoyqI&t=1s.

2   PCA Women's Ministry Trainers. *Thinking Biblically and Living Covenantally: A Biblical Apologetic for Women* (Lawrenceville, GA: Committee on Discipleship Ministries, 2014, 2017, 2018, 2019), 77.

3   William Hendrikson and Simon J. Kistemaker. *New Testament Commentary of Thessalonians, the Pastorals, and Hebrews* (Ada, MI: Baker Books, 1996), 339.

4   Susan Hunt, *Titus 2 Tools* (Lawrenceville, GA: PCA Committee on Discipleship Ministries, 2016).

Chapter 8

Everybody Plays the Fool: Discipling Women from Foolishness to Wisdom

K.A. Ellis

"GET WISDOM, GET UNDERSTANDING"

One of the most challenging parts of women's ministry today is discipleship. I often hear young women expressing their longing to be discipled, but they are unable to find a willing partner who isn't too tired or busy with the contours of her own life.

I can sympathize with these unmet longings. In the absence of a godly mentor, my own early discipling was haphazard at best, and my years as a young Christian were spent bumbling about, unlearning thoughts and behavior that had become second nature to existing in a fallen world.

When I finally did find a godly woman willing to spend the time, like many who converted to Christianity as adults, my first years of being discipled were based on fulfilling checklists of do's and don'ts and filling in the blanks of prescribed "one-size-fits-some" study books. At first, following the checklists appealed to my self-righteous nature. It felt good to tick off the boxes of righteousness as I strove to "be good," but I realized that I simply could not "be good" in my own strength, and on the road to maturity in Christ, I, like others, made regrettable choices that produced destruction rather than the wisdom that God intended.

I often think that if someone had explained the reasons *why* certain behaviors were associated with peace of mind, and if those "whys" hadn't been lost amidst endless "oughts," I might have left fewer messes in my wake.

As I mature in grace to disciple younger women, I now include teaching a biblical understanding of *why* a Christ-follower should move from foolishness to wisdom, from chaos to shalom.

How can we equip women in our church (including new believers and even those who are not yet believers) to understand the depth of shalom that humankind enjoyed in the Garden and better anticipate the deep shalom that those in Christ will know in the sweet by-and-by even as we live in nasty now-and-now?

"PLAYING THE FOOL"

Foolishness has been with us for a long time. Back in the 70s, the Motown group, The Main Ingredient, sang a song with this homespun truth:

Everybody plays the fool, sometimes . . .
There's no exception to the rule (listen baby!).
It may be factual, it may be cruel, (I ain't lying),
Everybody plays the fool.[1]

And yet, before there was foolishness, *Wisdom was.*

Proverbs tells us that "The LORD by Wisdom founded the earth; by understanding he established the heavens; by his knowledge the deeps broke open, and the clouds drop down the dew" (3:19-20). While Proverbs teaches that Christ created the universe by Wisdom, understanding and knowledge, the apostle Paul points out that the uncreated Christ Himself is our Wisdom (1 Cor. 1:18-31).

While the Bible speaks of Wisdom as a Person, it also speaks of wisdom as an asset—a benefit to life, created by Christ at the foundation of the world. In Proverbs 8, Wisdom's voice declares:

"The LORD possessed me at the beginning of his work,
the first of his acts of old.
Ages ago I was set up,
at the first, before the beginning of the earth" (Prov. 8:22-23).

The voice uses the rest of Chapter 8 to tell us the myriad ways that Wisdom existed before "Let us make," and before

"Let there be," and that it was *by the joyful power of Wisdom* that the world was ordered.

Let's continue to think of Wisdom both as a *Person* (Christ), and as a *force* used by that Person to create the first heaven and earth and to impart some very important information to the first man and woman.

Wisdom's imprint on us is a part of God's Garden package that shapes not only who we are, but why we were created and how we are to live. By dwelling with Wisdom in the Person of Christ, by whom, in whom, and through whom all things were made, Adam and Eve, our first parents, relied on Him to explain their world. They were to pattern themselves after His image by understanding the world through His eyes and living according to His ways.

Genesis 1:26-28 reminds us that on the sixth day, "Then God said, 'Let us make man *in our image,* after our likeness . . .'"—Adam, first out of the dust, and Eve, next out of his side. Bible commentator Matthew Henry points out that among all the non-human creatures of which God made many couples, man is the only one where he fashioned two out of one.[2] The man *and* the woman were a physical extension of the relational intimacy of the Trinity's creative force. This commonality has been described as God's image upon man— the imprint of Wisdom—consisting of three aspects: (1) *in knowledge,* Adam and Woman's ability to see divine things clearly and truly, (2) *in righteousness*, in that they complied readily and completely with the will of God, and (3) *in true holiness* (Eph. 4:24; Col. 3:10; Eccl. 7:29).[3]

This imprint of Wisdom applied creates the by-product *shalom,* a peaceful existence marked by three distinct blessings: *presence*, where God dwelt with man; *provision,* in a brand new, unspoiled heaven and earth; and *peace,* harmony with each other and the world around them. The Garden was created to be their sanctuary, their safe and protected dwelling place.

In some circles, the word "flourishing" has become an empty concept, co-opted more by self-fulfillment and gratification rather than dwelling in God's presence. But flourishing according to God's intentions for humanity is an important part of the "very good" of Garden life—a biblical concept that focuses on God-fulfillment rather than self. There were no hindrances to the first humans understanding God's world, His intentions, or His purposes, all through His eyes. Shalom—or flourishing—was and still is dwelling with Wisdom Himself, and it's directly tied to obedience to the Source of Wisdom. In the Garden, everything was designed to bring and preserve life. It was, as the Creator declared, very good.

But it was not yet perfect, as we soon see in the story . . . perfection would be reserved for glory.

SEE, WHAT HAD HAPPENED WAS . . .

Often in the style of African-American storytelling, when we want to explain how a bad thing happened, we begin with the words *"See, what had happened was . . ."* The hearer's ears are pricked by this grammatically-challenged preamble, as it always introduces the moment when everything that is right goes wrong.

Such a preamble is appropriate here as Satan, the Purveyor of Chaos, slithers into our peaceful picture.

Isaiah 14:12-14 tells us that Satan ruined himself by desiring to be like the Most High: "How you are fallen from heaven, O Day Star, son of Dawn! How you are cut down to the ground, who laid the nations low! You said in your heart, 'I will ascend to heaven; above the stars of God I will set my throne on high; I will sit on the mount of assembly in the far reaches of the north; I will ascend above the heights of the clouds; I will make myself like the Most High.'" This was ambition at its most foolish, an attempt at an act which could never be attained.

The one who could not bear to dwell with the Prince of Peace convinced the woman that the tree of the knowledge of good and evil—the tree that had been forbidden by God "—was good for food, and that it was a delight to the eyes, *and that the tree was to be desired to make one wise*, she took of its fruit and ate, and she also gave some to her husband who was with her, and he ate" (Gen. 3:6).

How ironic that Wisdom is included in the deception! They were already wise, since they walked and dwelt with Wisdom Himself. Wisdom was the first and natural orientation of Adam and Eve in the Garden, but they chose instead to dwell with foolishness, and we, as their descendants, dwell with foolishness as well.

Obedience is the component in personal Wisdom, based on knowledge of *how* we were created (by a God of order and life), *for the purpose* (to bring glory and honor to God), that produces shalom. It is obedience that puts the life force in Wisdom, and the result of disobedience and the abandonment of Wisdom and shalom is reported in Romans 1:21-23: "For although they knew God, they did not honor him as God or give thanks to him, but they became futile in their thinking, and their foolish hearts were darkened. Claiming to be wise, they became fools, and exchanged the glory of the immortal God for images resembling mortal man and birds and animals and creeping things."

Figure 1: The Exchange

Wisdom →Obedience →Shalom	Foolishness →Disappointment →Chaos
• Relationship	• Brokenness
• Affection	• Resentment
• Harmony w/ Creation	• Disharmony w/ Creation
• Trust	• Doubt
• Unity	• Discord
• Agreement	• Discrepancy
• Security	• Danger
• Balance	• Oppression
• Abundance	• Paucity

Imagine the first couple experiencing never-before-known emotions of fear and shame cascading down through their souls, after knowing only pure and sweet shalom!

Indeed, foolishness was not a part of the created order and was never intended for their good; it was forced upon them by a hostile entity, bent on shattering their God-given shalom.

Put another way, Wisdom and truth brought peace and harmony; folly and lies brought chaos and disorder, a principle still at work in the world today.

"TWO HOUSES, UNALIKE IN DIGNITY"

At the fall, the tuition for forsaking biblical Wisdom became astronomically high. Yet, throughout Proverbs and the rest of Scripture, Christ's breath of life, Wisdom, presence-dwelling and shalom, continues to be a life-giving force wherever it's found.

Solomon—the man who prized Wisdom above all else—and other contributors to the Wisdom sayings, give us a view of this costly exchange. Still in view is the notion that when you seek Wisdom, you seek God Himself, and that there is life at the end of each moment of pursuit. Just as in the Garden, we have two possible orientations: Wisdom leading to life or folly leading to death.

Ironically, the contrast between wise and foolish choices and the consequences of each and the quality of peace we experience based on what we choose are laced throughout Scripture. Every choice made by our Scriptural ancestors is a choice between Wisdom that leads to life and foolishness that leads to death.

Chapter 3 of Proverbs prepares us for this discourse and gives us a snapshot of the personal results of seeking Wisdom. Keep the events of Genesis 3 in mind as you read these verses, and they will drip with knowledge and regret over what was lost:

Trust in the LORD with all your heart, and do lean not on your own understanding. In all your ways, acknowledge him, and he will make straight your paths. Be not wise in your own eyes; fear the LORD and turn away from evil. It will be healing to your flesh and refreshment to your bones (vv. 5-8).

In the following chapters, Proverbs outlines the application and benefits of Wisdom to specific areas of our lives in contrast with the consequences of foolishness. In chapter 8, something very exciting begins to unfold.

Proverbs 8 and 9 frame the created asset of Wisdom in the feminine, as well as her opposite force—foolishness. Here, we have two options: two women, two houses, two meals, and the connection between *presence, provision and peace* continues only in Wisdom's house. Her home is built

on seven pillars, and since seven is a sacred and complete
concept, the house in which she dwells is the image of
a peaceful world. The writer of the Proverb personifies
Wisdom and Folly in the feminine, tying them both to
Woman's choices in the Garden.

Which of these two houses is the dwelling that will lead
to the shalom intended in that first Garden shelter, where the
first tempting bite threw the world off kilter?

Let's look at the two side by side:

Figure 2. Two Houses[4]

WISDOM'S HOUSE	FOLLY'S HOUSE
• Wisdom invites the simple – those who lack judgment. • Wisdom has maids: a spirit of cooperation and community; the guests are robust and full of life. • The meal is planned. • Her way requires repentance— turning from the simple ways. • The intimate knowledge of God is the doorway to life. • Wisdom offers a sumptuous banquet. The meat and wine represent the good teaching of Wisdom that will be palatable (tasty) and profitable (healthy), foreshadowing the flesh and blood of Jesus (John 6:56). • Wisdom is open about her table. • Wisdom offers lasting reward; gracious words are like a honeycomb, sweetness to the soul and health to the body (Prov. 3:8, 3:22, 8:35, 16:24).	• Folly parrots Wisdom in her invitation, just as the serpent parroted God in the Garden; *"You will not surely die..."* • She has no attendants, and her guests are the dead, those who have rejected the straight path that leads to Wisdom's home. • Her hospitality lacks discipline. • Her way requires no transformation. • There's no knowledge of God provided. • Folly's meal—water and bread—is stolen. • Folly eats in secret. • No life-giving nourishment can be found in Folly's house —not even the smallest morsel.

Moreover, it's a grace of God that Wisdom can be ours, no matter what the externals of our lives; she holds her invitation out to all. Wisdom doesn't stipulate, "If you're married or single, if you have a quiver-full of children or none, you will be wise." Wisdom doesn't call only if you're male or female, young or old, tall, short, White, Hispanic, Black, or Asian. Wisdom makes no external requirements; she simply beckons all to "come, and live," and it's through union with Christ—Wisdom Himself—that we find our way back to covenant peace and shalom.

A question for ourselves then, and for those whom we disciple is, "In which house, and with whom, do we want to spend our days?"

"THE ETERNAL HOUSE OF WISDOM"

Revelation 21 and 22 whet our appetite for dwelling eternally in Wisdom's house. What awaits us there? Again, the motif of presence, provision and peace reveals itself.

The apostle John writes of our eternal home in the best of human terms. It's grand and fortified with high and strong walls. It's a safe and protected place, and just as in Wisdom's house in Proverbs, there are guests and there is a meal.

This is the place Christ Himself has gone to prepare for His people (John 14:1-14), just as He lovingly crafted a place for us at Creation. In the revelation, the three basic blessings of the Garden become our glorified reality.

In *Presence*, now the dwelling of God is with man and the covenant promise is restated and fulfilled: *He will be our God and we will be His people* (Rev. 21:3, 7). In God's *Provision*, we now occupy the New Heaven and New Earth (Rev. 21:1-2). In *Peace*, He wipes every tear from our eyes in this fortified and protected city (Rev. 21:12-14, 25).

We are no longer merely inhabiting a garden; there's an entire new city in view. Justice and mercy have been dispensed, and the serpent of foolishness, lies, and destruction, which had become a full-blown dragon tormenting the nations, will never enter; Christ has accomplished what Adam did not, so no unclean or accursed thing will ever enter these fortified walls (Rev. 21:27).

Just as it was described at Wisdom's house in Proverbs, we have a banquet within these walls of safety—the marriage supper of the Lamb, in the presence of Christ Himself. The Tree of Life provides twelve different fruits, springing from one tree, such is the abundance! Nothing is wasted in this economy— even the leaves are useful for the healing of the nations.

Presence, Provision, and Peace . . .

Shalom.

"WISDOM IN THE NASTY NOW-AND-NOW"

We began our discussion asking the question: as we wait for the sweet by-and-by, how do we apply Wisdom and help women we disciple find shalom, even as we live in the nasty now-and-now?

God proves with each generation through Scripture that He will keep His covenant promises, even when we are foolish and disobedient. However, His covenant-keeping does not absolve us of our responsibility to obedience or to the exercise of Wisdom according to His Word. At any given time, we are either moving toward life, or we're moving toward death. Paul further qualifies the foundation of these two poles by framing them in Romans 6 as "dead to sin" or "alive in Christ."

We've not been left floating haphazardly in a world of foolishness and chaos. As we anticipate glory, we're told that the Holy Spirit will guide us into all *knowledge and Wisdom* (John 16:13). The people of God must walk together knowing that in every age, lasting peace is only built on Wisdom's foundation.

In our current age of moral relativism, it's imperative that we ground ourselves in Truth. As we disciple those God loves, the question "Is this course of action wise?" seems to go hand in hand with questions of right and wrong. Biblical Wisdom, when pursued in the community of the local church and applied to all areas of life, has the potential to produce good and reliable Christians and to produce holiness in them. Of course, in times of persecution and anti-Christian hostility, the choice to follow Christ's ways may lead to destruction of our physical bodies, but such choices based on obedience to His Word that place us in the fellowship of His sufferings will never lead to the destruction of our souls.

In applying redemptive Wisdom to life's tricky concerns, we cannot fear sharing our own stories with the women we disciple and telling them about God redeeming our own foolish and destructive life choices. Because we all know the compelling call of foolishness, we cannot be afraid to risk a relationship to say, "This path is destruction. This path is life." Waiting prayerfully for loved ones to turn from foolishness preserves both our love and our hope.

I also try to keep in mind that we are all attempting the decades-long road of discipleship in a microwave-oven world. How much pressure does my own impatience exert when I demand a new convert show an instant and seemingly perfect desire for a sacrificial life that honors God above all? Yet as we walk alongside with prayer and long-suffering and do not give up, we display our own belief in the Lord's promise that He who has begun a good work in each of us will faithfully complete that work until the day we are all perfected in His presence.

Fig. 3: Walking Out Wisdom in Discipleship Communities

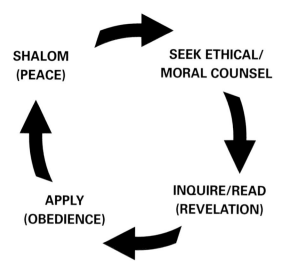

SHALOM (PEACE)

SEEK ETHICAL/ MORAL COUNSEL

INQUIRE/READ (REVELATION)

APPLY (OBEDIENCE)

Because of the creative work of Christ, shalom was our right in the Garden, yet stolen from us by the enemy of shalom.

Because of the redemptive work of Christ and through His obedience, shalom and the peace that passes all understanding is a present right for all who have inclined their hearts to Him as the ultimate Source of Wisdom. Through the work of the now glorified Christ, we will dwell—this time, undisturbed in the new heaven and the new earth.

This is the restorative work of Wisdom . . . this is the redemptive work of Christ.

K.A. Ellis holds a Master of Art in Religion from Westminster Theological Seminary, an MFA from the Yale School of Drama, and is a PhD candidate in Virtue Ethics at the Oxford Center for Mission Studies in England. In 2017, she was named Robert Cannada Fellow for World Christianity by Reformed Theological Seminary.

DISCUSSION QUESTIONS

1. What Scriptures exemplify the long wait for a rebellious person to realize her own foolishness? Discuss the perspective of both sides: the one waiting for the prodigal to return, and the one in rebellion.

2. Sometimes foolish choices aren't driven by direct rebellion, but rather by learned cultural patterns. While Christ may be glorified by some cultural tendencies, He longs to set us free from dysfunctional cultural tendencies that dishonor His creation. Discuss how dysfunctional patterns (such as instant gratification leading to poor financial priorities, bigamy, racism or cultural elitism, holding a low view of human life, upholding dehumanizing behavior as heroic, or the like) can underlie foolish/destructive decisions. How should we apply biblical Wisdom and model an alternative Kingdom-oriented culture, particularly when discipling in cross-cultural situations?

3. Who among our Scriptural ancestors has a story that reflects God's redemption of foolish and destructive

choices? Consider the times when God has redeemed your own foolish and destructive choices. Draw and share from your own history, not the histories of others.

1   The Main Ingredient, "Everybody Plays the Fool," by J.R. Bailey, Rudy Clark, and Ken Williams, recorded August 1972, track 4 on *Bitter Sweet*, RCA's Studio C, 33 1/3 rpm.
2   F.R. Hist and Leslie F. Church (eds.), *Matthew Henry's Commentary in One Volume: Genesis to Revelation* (Grand Rapids, MI.: Zondervan, 1999), 18-23.
3   G. I. Williamson, *The Westminster Confession of Faith for Study Classes*, 2nd ed. (Phillipsburg, N.J: P & R Pub, 2004), Chapter 4.2, Part Two.
4   Adapted from Frank E. Gaebelein (ed.) *The Expositor's Bible Commentary: With the New International Version of the Holy Bible; in 12 Vol. 5: Psalms - Song of Songs*. 2. print. (Grand Rapids, MI: Regency Reference Library, 1991), 943-950.

Part Two

Facing Issues in 21st Century Ministry

Chapter 9

The Gospel: "Fighting Words"
Abby Hutto

I f asked a decade ago if I knew and understood the gospel,
I would have indignantly rolled my eyes and said, "Of course
I do!" As a Director of Women's Ministry, I felt confident
that I knew the gospel, yet my life told a different story. I was
critical, easily frustrated, prone to angry outbursts at home, and
suffering from exhaustion. Though I was able to give a gospel
presentation to someone, I was not living as if the gospel had
anything to do with my everyday life.

Now, after ten years of serving in the local church, I
can say with confidence that what I knew about the gospel
when I began wasn't nearly enough. Over the years, my own
inadequacies, failures, and inconsistencies have pushed
me to dig deeper into this "basic" concept. I have found it
to be incredibly complex and nuanced, holding the power
of salvation for every situation I face because it reveals the
character and nature of God to me.

For more than ten years, I have seen this power at work in
our community. The gospel has transformed broken marriages
and given women the courage to bring long-held secrets into
the light. It has equipped mothers to generously love wayward
children. I have seen it strengthen women in the trenches
who are battling mental illness, depression, and fatigue. The
gospel has held women together who have buried loved ones
as they place their hope in the Resurrected One. And the
greatest miracle of all, I experienced the gospel transform my
hardened, unforgiving, critical heart and give me back the
joy of my salvation. The gospel is truly the power of God for
salvation to everyone who believes (Rom. 1:16).

Because the "gospel" is a word that is commonly used in churches today, we operate under the assumption that we all know what it means. However, if you asked women to explain what the gospel means or why it matters, you'd find that many would struggle to give you an answer. You might get the definition "good news" (which it is), but how many could articulate why the news of the gospel is so good and why it is necessary to believe in our darkest moments? What does the gospel have to do with my struggle to forgive? How does the gospel impact how I view my relationships, work, health, and finances? How does it motivate me to obey God's commands? These are questions that most women don't even know to ask.

How many of the women in your church would speak about the gospel as "fighting words"—the weapon they use to fight back the lies of the enemy, the darkness of sin, the despair that creeps in the corners of their hearts? I believe we fail to grasp the potency of the gospel, and in doing so, neglect to apply its truths to the very situations where we need its "fighting words" the most. It is important that we teach our women the essence of what this "good news" tells us. To help the women in our church understand these issues, we must first ask ourselves these questions: What is the gospel? How might I fail to apply it to my life and in my ministry? How can and should it empower me to fight against sin, Satan, and the brokenness of life?

WHAT IS THE GOSPEL?

It is important to define what we mean by "the gospel." The word means "good news"—a declaration of something that has already happened. Jesus began His ministry by preaching a simple sermon, "The time is fulfilled, and the kingdom of God is at hand; repent and believe in the gospel" (Mark 1:15). What is the "good news" that we are called to believe?

Many people begin defining the gospel with the death of Jesus, but in reality, the gospel is a plan that was in place before mankind even existed (Eph. 1:4). God created us, knowing that we would rebel against Him, reject His love, and wreck His world (2 Tim. 1:9; Titus 1:2-3). God did not orchestrate our salvation as a "Divine Plan B." The gospel was always the plan, even though saving His wayward children would come at a terrible cost for God.

The gospel tells us that the Father looked down on a broken world, in active rebellion against Him and, instead of responding with wrath that annihilated us, *He loved us* (John 3:16; Rom. 5:8). He gave us His only beloved Son, wrapped in the frailty of human flesh. Jesus lived like us in every way so that He could sympathize with our weaknesses (Heb. 4:14-15). This love compelled Jesus to live a perfectly obedient life, even when obedience led Him to a cross (Phil. 2:8).

At the cross we see the ultimate expression of the costly love of God. The perfect Son laid down His life, accepting the punishment we deserve, so that you and I could be brought back to the loving arms of the Father (1 Peter 2:24). The resurrection proves that the sacrifice of Jesus was accepted, and we are now counted as righteous (Eph. 2:4-6). The Holy Spirit, who resides in every believer, continually unpacks the gospel for us, applying its truth to every aspect of our lives, sanctifying us for this beautiful kingdom of God (1 Cor. 6:19-20; John 14:26; Eph. 5:16-24).

We are so deeply loved by the Father, Son, and Holy Spirit that they would enter into suffering to draw us close to themselves. This is what Jesus is asking us to respond to. Repent of the sin and the rebellion that separates you from this incredible love. Believe that God is who He says He is and will accomplish what He promises to do in you. Give your life to a kingdom that is fighting back darkness, a kingdom that will never end. This is the gospel!

LEARNING TO APPLY THE GOSPEL

Every aspect of life provides us the opportunity to repent and believe the gospel. I had to learn how to apply the gospel to my view of ministry. For many years, I assessed my success in ministry by numbers. How many women were involved in Bible studies? Were events well-attended? Was the women's ministry drawing people to the church? None of these questions are bad in and of themselves, but I allowed numbers to affect how I viewed myself. I felt great when the numbers swelled. When they lagged, I began to question my gifts, abilities, and even my calling. This roller coaster of emotions was exhausting.

One event forced me to honestly assess my failure to apply the gospel in this area of my life. I planned our first ever "Women's Ministry Kick-Off." Our leaders set up booths showcasing how women could get involved. After several hours preparing, we expected a big turnout. But when we opened the doors, no one showed up! As the night dragged on and only a couple of ladies trickled in, I felt the rising tide of anxiety. This event was a flop! As I looked around the room and saw the discomfort of the other leaders, I felt the heat of embarrassment creeping up my face. The accusations of the enemy whispered to me, "You should give this whole ministry thing up and go home. You are a failure."

I knew in that moment I had a choice. I could either continue to judge my entire value and worth in ministry by the numbers, or I could choose to believe and apply the gospel. What did the gospel tell me was true? The weight of the Church sits squarely on Jesus' shoulders, not mine. He is the hero of their stories, not me. The Holy Spirit will mature His daughters, and their salvation and growth will happen with or without me. And the same Father who loved me while I was His enemy, loves and delights in me still, no matter how many dud events I plan! He called me to this ministry, and He will equip me to do it. I cannot lose His love or delight in me as His child. I fought the lies of the enemy with this truth, "I am not a failure—I am God's treasure."

Relief washed over me as I rehearsed these truths. The Holy Spirit gently showed me that for far too long, I judged myself by the wrong standards. I felt genuine grief as He revealed that I brought an intensity to our ministry that was a burden to the women I led. That evening, I gathered the leaders together to process what it felt like to have only five women show up to an event. I encouraged them with the truths the Spirit had reminded me of: God is pleased with us simply because we are His children. I am genuinely thankful that the event flopped, because it gave us all an opportunity to believe the gospel.

That experience changed the course of our women's

ministry. We became far more interested in seeing women grow in their understanding of God's love than we were with the numbers. When that became our passion, we changed as leaders, and the focus of our ministry changed. Through the work of the Spirit, this church is now full of women who believe the gospel and love the God that accomplished it. They are women who preach the gospel to their own hearts in everyday situations and fight back sin and the accusations of the enemy with the knowledge of the character and nature of their God.

BECOMING A GOSPEL PREACHER

To truly apply the gospel to every aspect of life, we need to become gospel preachers. The gospel must become our "fighting words" that we wield against our insecurities, doubts, and fears. In his book, *Spiritual Depression,* D.M. Lloyd-Jones calls this "knowing how to handle yourself." He talks about preaching a three-point gospel sermon to your struggling soul when you are overcome by discouragement: Who God is, what God has already done, and what God has pledged to do for you. He goes on to say, "Then, having done that, end on this great note: defy yourself, and defy other people, and defy the devil and the whole world [by saying] . . . Hope thou in God, for I shall yet praise him."[1] Only those who see the love of God displayed in the gospel have the fighting words they need to defy the destructive voices that surround us. Only the gospel can compel us to preach the character and nature of God in the face of our discouragement.

Over the past decade, I have learned that the gospel is not something I will ever grow out of, because at the heart of the gospel is a person. Best-selling author and pastor, Tim Keller, once said, "The gospel doesn't just come through Jesus Christ, it IS Jesus Christ."[2] The life, death, and resurrection of Jesus Christ prove the love and power of God, and these are the fighting words I need to beat back the accusations of the enemy and defeat the siren call of sin. The more I understand the love of the Father, Son, and Holy Spirit, the more I rejoice in the truth of the gospel and long for it to permeate every aspect of my heart and life.

We will never outgrow our need for the gospel, because we can never outgrow the Trinity. Their love surrounds us, defends us, upholds us, sanctifies us, and carries us until the end. *All of God is for me.* Who cares who is against me (my paraphrase of Rom. 8:31)?! These are our "fighting words," the sermon we preach, applying this gospel to every aspect of life until we reach Glory. When faith becomes sight, we will enter into the fullness of their love for all eternity. This is the gospel.

Abby Hutto is the Director of Spiritual Formation at Story Presbyterian Church in Westerville, Ohio, and works for Parakaleo, a ministry that provides support and resources to women in church planting. She is the author of *God for Us: Discovering the Heart of the Father Through the Life of the Son* (P&R Publishing, 2019).

DISCUSSION QUESTIONS

1. What situations do you encounter in life where you struggle to believe and/or apply the truth of the gospel?

2. What truths do you need to be reminded of when you struggle? Truths about who God is; what He has already done; what He has promised to do?

3. Compile a list of "Fighting Words" that you can take with you into battle with the enemy or when you are tempted to sin. How could you help others compile their own lists?

1   D. Martyn Lloyd-Jones, *Spiritual Depression, Its Causes and Cure* (Grand Rapids, MI: Wm. B. Eerdmans Publishing Co., 2001), 21.
2   Tim Keller, "The Gospel-Shaped Life from 50,000 Feet." Audio blog post. The Gospel Coalition Orange County Regional Conference. The Gospel Coalition, 9 March 2018. Web. 11 June 2018.

Chapter 10

A Diversity of Friendships
Maria Garriott

"We want our ministry to be diverse," women say, "but that hasn't happened. How do we reach people from different backgrounds, races, and classes?"

We know the gospel transcends all boundaries, but often our churches and ministries don't reflect this. Because many new church attendees come at the invitation of a friend, a better question might be, "How do we encourage women to pursue diverse relationships?"

Several years ago, when I went to retrieve my car from a downtown underground parking garage after a meeting, I couldn't find it—the garage, not the car. I retraced my steps through steaming city streets for over an hour, increasingly confused and frustrated. "Who loses an entire parking *garage?*"

Finally, I walked into a local nonprofit and confessed my plight. The employees pulled out a map, and one staffer offered to drive me around. Then, as if by divine summons, a long-time church member walked by.

"Jim!" I called. As we embraced like old friends, the staffer looked on curiously. Why was this professionally-dressed Caucasian woman hugging an African-American man in work boots and paint-splattered overalls? "This is my friend from church!" I explained. Jim volunteered to drive me around in his truck and reunite me with my car.

Sometimes, people are curious when diverse groups from my church eat out together. "So, how do you all know each other? Do you work together?" waitresses ask. After all, what could a young Korean guy, a middle-aged African-American woman, a balding white guy, and the thirty-something Latina have in common?

We have Jesus in common.

Because most American churches have struggled to embrace the diversity in their regions, the decades-old fellowship I've enjoyed with people from different ethnic, racial, or socio-economic backgrounds is, sadly, too rare. Sixty years after Martin Luther King, Jr. found it "appalling" that Sunday morning was "the most segregated hour of Christian America," that is largely still true.[1] LifeWay Research recently found that more than eight in ten congregations were composed of one predominant racial group, yet less than half of churchgoers think their church should become more diverse. Ed Stetzer, executive director of LifeWay Research, said, "Surprisingly, most churchgoers are content with the ethnic status quo . . . In a world where our culture is increasingly diverse . . . it appears most people are happy where they are—and with whom they are. Yet, it's hard for Christians to say they are united in Christ when they are congregating separately."[2]

When my husband and I moved into an under-resourced neighborhood to start an intentionally multi-ethnic church in hyper-segregated Baltimore in 1980, people thought this was an unrealistic, impractical dream. It was—outside of Christ, but we have reaped the benefits of learning from people with varied backgrounds and stories. Our lives—and the lives of our children—have been deeply shaped and enriched by these relationships.

In the past, Caucasian-Americans could survive without understanding and interacting sensitively with other cultures, while African-Americans, Native Americans, Latinos, Asian-Americans, and others *had* to "codeswitch" and be culturally bilingual. America is changing. Half of American children under one year of age are now people of color;[3] by 2045, Anglos will no longer be the majority.[4] Because God has brought the nations to our shores, obeying the Great Commission and reaching all *ethnos* can often begin in our own neighborhoods.

Jesus reconciles us to God, but also to one another as part of God's universal, diverse "beloved community." Our adoption as sons and daughters becomes our primary identity, superseding other identities. When Paul told the Galatians that there was neither Jew nor Greek, slave nor free, male nor female, "for you are all one in Christ Jesus" (Gal. 3:28), he was not erasing gender or ethnic distinctions; he was highlighting their surpassing unity. Jesus created "one new humanity" out of the Jew and Gentile (Eph. 2:14-16). Paul describes it as a "mystery" that once-estranged ethnic groups are now "members of the same body" (Eph. 3:6). Just as a nonbiological child is embraced and enfolded into a family, we are adopted into God's diverse family.

Jesus promised that the unity of His followers would testify to His divinity. In His final high priestly prayer, He prayed for their unity "so that the world may believe that you have sent me" (John 17). When outsiders see this unity, they take note. In *The Rise of Christianity,* religion sociologist Rodney Stark notes that the early church—unlike other religious groups—was racially integrated, and that this contributed to Christianity's rapid spread.[5] Commenting on this racial harmony, author J.D. Greear writes, "The world saw that Jesus was not just a Jewish king or regional god."[6]

A Quaker friend from my exercise class visited our church with her special-needs adult son. As she introduced me to a non-religious friend of hers later, she marveled at the unity she'd seen. "Their church is the most diverse church you could imagine! And people have been so welcoming to our son."

I need diverse relationships across the divides of class, race, and ethnicity for my own sanctification and to develop a more biblical worldview. We tend to love—and be most comfortable with—people who think like us, vote like us, and spend like us. It's easy. Yet diverse friendships help me evaluate my own culture under the lens of Scripture. Culture—values, behaviors, ways of thinking and behaving—is so deeply rooted that we often fail to see it. Yet culture dramatically impacts our faith. Missiologist David Livermore finds that American ministry leaders "have limited awareness of how significantly culture shapes the way one reads the Bible."[7]

One year, my daughter Caroline brought an international student home from college for Christmas. Although the girl's family was wealthy enough to fund her study abroad, I was acutely conscious of the materialism of an American Christmas—even our relatively humble one. I wondered how this looked in her eyes.

I work with Parakaleo, a ministry that supports church-planting spouses with training, coaching, and local or virtual network groups. As we train women from China, Australia, Singapore, Latin America, and the U.S., we form deep relationships across national and cultural boundaries. The struggles faced by women in ministry—and the power of the gospel—transcend these divides.

As part of my six-week online Parakaleo class, "A Gospel Lens Look at Developing Cultural Intelligence," participants discuss a video clip that replicates a famous 1950s experiment in which children were shown two identical dolls, one black and one white. When asked which doll was "nice," "bad," "ugly," or "pretty," they overwhelmingly identified the black dolls as "bad" or "ugly." In 2010, CNN redid this experiment using cartoon images of children with skin tones ranging from white to dark. When asked which child was ugly, bad, or dumb, both the white and the African-American children pointed to the darkest image.[8] As my cohort participants watched the video, I could see their faces via our online platform. Shock, grief, outrage, and even revulsion registered on the five white participants. The African-American woman cried and walked away from the screen. "I'm thinking about my grandchildren," she said. The Caucasian women saw aspects of their culture they'd never fully understood before. The African-American woman saw how racism could affect her grandchildren.

Befriending people who aren't like me is both challenging and enriching. While facts may lodge in our heads, lessons with a human face are indelibly imprinted in our hearts. Early in our ministry, I befriended a neighbor who funded her drug addiction by working as an exotic dancer. Her trajectory to addiction, abuse, the sex trade, and prison had begun in middle school and included family trauma and sexual abuse. I experienced the limitations and hard realities of loving someone in the throes of addiction.

Like all relationships, friendships across divides require intentionality, patience, and nurture in the midst of already-busy lives. Once, when an immigrant friend and I stopped into a convenience store, she heard the clerk speak in her native language and struck up a conversation. My friend told the clerk she'd been in the country three years. The clerk looked at us. "I've been here seven years. I still don't have any white friends." No white Christians had obeyed the call to "welcome the stranger"? No white Christians had seen their own culture through her eyes? No Caucasians had shared Jesus or a Fourth of July cookout or a Christmas Eve service with her?

At my local YMCA, I met a recent immigrant and her daughters and invited them to dinner. They had come to America from a Muslim country so their daughters could pursue an education. My friend had a master's degree, but because her English was poor and she lacked a driver's license, the only work she could find was at a convenience store. I helped her navigate bureaucracy and learn to drive. Another church member advocated for and tutored the middle daughter, who nearly dropped out of high school because of depression. A woman from a nearby church let this family live in her basement apartment for a year to save money to buy a house. The oldest daughter is now entering medical school. Although my friend and one daughter made faith commitments, they fell away after the family stabilized. But only God knows what seeds have been planted. What did I gain? I gained a friend. I saw aspects of her culture that I wished to emulate, and others I didn't. I recognized how hard it is to navigate a new language and culture. I learned again how easy it is to take too much responsibility and play the "savior" because—well, I speak my native tongue, and understand American culture.

Diverse friendships enrich us with unique gifts—and I don't just mean Korean bulgogi, Mexican tortillas, or Hungarian goulash—I mean the life experiences and cultural perspectives that make me think. The more I learn about America's "original sin" of slavery and the system of white supremacy it established, the more humbled I am by the patience and long-suffering of the African-American church. Sadly, Asian-American history is rife with anti-immigrant bias; consider the Chinese Exclusion Act (1882) and the internment of Japanese-American citizens during World War II. As our nation becomes increasingly secular and hostile to Christianity, those who experienced the crucible of suffering can teach us. Theologian Thabiti Anyabwile says evangelicals can "learn to be the moral minority from a much older moral minority."[9] As we see others suffer with dignity and grace, we learn to hope in God more fully.

My friend Erin, who survived a traumatic car accident, lives a joy-filled, ministry-focused life while hounded by chronic pain. Another friend uncomplainingly takes care of her disabled adult daughter. My friend JoAnna serves with her pastor-husband in a ministry to the homeless and lives with her family of six in a 900-square-feet house. My friend Vernette is a 70-something prayer warrior who raised four young grandchildren after she turned fifty. These friends give me perspective when I want to complain about my troubles.

In Revelation, we learn that Jesus "ransomed people for God from every tribe and language and people and nation" (Rev. 5:9). The apostle John saw "a great multitude . . . from all tribes and peoples and languages" worshiping (Rev. 7:9). Together, we reflect the vastness of God's Creation and Kingdom and experience a foretaste of heaven.

So how do we—and the women we lead in our churches— reach out across dividing lines? Pray for God's leading. Take the first step in your neighborhood, school, workplace, or grocery store. Have a humble, teachable spirit; no one wants to be your "project" or token friend. Be intentional and curious. Listen to the stories and concerns of other races and ethnic groups and women from different socio-economic groups. Anticipate hardships; cross-cultural experiences create disequilibrium because they take us out of our comfort zone. You will make mistakes, but don't give up on building cross-cultural relationships.

Here's the best part: the gospel enables us to risk rejection, persevere when we feel weak, examine our sin and blindness, forgive those who wound us, and ask others for forgiveness. We can face our sins without self-condemnation, remembering that Jesus paid for them. As we reflect on

Scripture and hear one another's stories, the Holy Spirit changes us. And as we develop a deeper love and appreciation for our brothers and sisters, we grow in our ability to proclaim and live out the gospel, our ministry reflects the diversity in heaven, and we become more like Jesus.

Maria Garriott is on staff with *Parakaleo*, a ministry to church-planting spouses, and is the author of *A Thousand Resurrections*, a memoir of urban church-planting.

DISCUSSION QUESTIONS

1. How did Jesus model diversity in His relationships?

2. What do you think will be the most challenging aspect of pursuing friendships across racial, ethnic, or socio-economic divides? What hinders or is scary to you about pursing these kinds of friendships?

3. What do you see as the blessings of pursuing diverse friendships?

4. How can your women's ministry proactively provide opportunities for women of different racial, ethnic, or socio-economic divides to develop friendships or discipleship relationships?

5. How is your women's ministry including mature Christian women of racial, ethnic, or socio-economic backgrounds into leadership positions in your ministry?

1   Martin Luther King, Jr. "Meet the Press." Filmed April 17, 1960. YouTube video, 1 minute. Posted April 29, 2014. https://www.youtube.com/watch?v=1q881g1L_d8.
2   "Sunday morning in America is still segregated—and that's OK with worshippers," LifeWay Research, Posted Jan 15, 2015. https://blog.lifeway.com/newsroom/2015/01/15/sunday-morning-in-america-still-segregated-and-thats-ok-with-worshipers/.
3   "Most Children Younger Than Age 1 are Minorities, Census Bureau Reports," U.S. Census Bureau, May 17, 2012, https://www.census.gov/newsroom/releases/archives/population/cb12-90.html
4   William Frey. "The U.S. Will Become 'Minority White' in 2045, Census Projects," The Brookings Institute, March 14, 2018, https://www.brookings.edu/blog/the-avenue/2018/03/14/the-us-will-become-minority-white-in-2045-census-projects/
5   David Murray. *The Happy Christian: Ten Ways to be a Joyful Believer in a Gloomy World*

(Nashville: Nelson Books, 2015), 213. Murray quotes Rodney Stark's *The Rise of Christianity*, (HarperCollins, 1997).

6 J.D. Greear, "Why Pursue Racial Integration in Our Churches (A Practical Answer), J.D. Greear Ministries, Posted March 11, 2013. *https://jdgreear.com/blog/why-pursue-racial-integration-in-our-churches-a-practical-answer.*

7 Murray, *The Happy Christian,* 147. Murray quotes David Livermore, *Cultural Intelligence: Improving Your CQ to Engage Our Multicultural World* (Grand Rapids: Baker Academic, 2009), 17.

8 "Study: White and Black Children are Biased Toward White Skin." CNN. http://www.cnn.com/2010/US/05/13/doll.study/index.html. May 14, 2010.

9 Thabiti Anyabwile. "Learning to be the Moral Minority from a Moral Minority," The Gospel Coalition, posted Feb 14, 2103. https://www.thegospelcoalition.org/blogs/thabiti-anyabwile/learning-to-be-the-moral-minority-from-a-moral-minority/.

Chapter 11

Rooted in the Gospel…Accessible for All?
Ashley Belknap

D isability ministry and women's ministry are entwined topics—both are committed to discipleship and fellowship—yet these two ministries very rarely converse. Often when we think of ministry to families who are touched by disability, we may initially think of children's ministry as the one on the front lines. Often, women within our women's ministries do come alongside young families impacted by disability, offering respite to parents, for example, or helping to make adaptations to Sunday school for their child. However, as these children grow into youth and then launch into the world of young adults and women's ministry, we slowly start to lose them, and therein, fail to enfold and disciple women with disabilities through their adult years at church.

National statistics show that one in four adults has some type of presenting disability. What about women in your congregation who have moved to the fringes due to the effects of depression, chronic illness, dementia, or bipolar disorder? Are women with intellectual disabilities members of your women's Bible studies? What about women with decreased mobility—are they as present and involved in church as they once were? And what about the young mom whose child has behavioral problems related to her disability—is she able to fully participate in church-body life?

Through my years of vocational ministry, I have served as both a director of women's ministry within a local church and as the director of a denominational disability ministry. I love women's ministry and I love disability ministry. Yet for the most part, I find that the two sides of ministry do not intersect except within a caregiving context. Women's ministries are often vibrant expressions of spiritual growth within churches, and disability ministries are often seeking the support needed for the families that they serve. What would happen if women's ministries embraced women with disabilities within their small group Bible studies, service ministries, and ministry lunches? What would happen if fully-abled women pursued genuine friendship with women with unique abilities? How would church body life change?

EMBRACING SIMILARITIES

I found joy in women's ministry where plans often came to quick fruition and where there were always many volunteers to help serve. When challenges arose, we did not have to significantly rethink or rework ministry plans in order to keep moving faithfully forward. This is in contrast to the creative confidence required to remain theologically sound while making adaptations that may seem way outside the box in order to reach, disciple, and enfold children, teens, and adults who have disabilities. Within disability ministry, answers are rarely clear-cut, and steps forward are often found through trial, error, and a great deal of love and patience.

In my days of women's ministry, I honestly thought very little about the women impacted by disability. I never looked at women's Bible studies and thought about who was missing because they intellectually, socially, or physically could not participate like the other women. I never thought about why I didn't know well the families who were touched by disability. I never thought about what hospitality might look like when extended in a way that would encourage and bring joy to those families impacted by disabilities. I saw families who had children with disabilities—I even knew them by name and tried to stop in the hallway for conversation when I saw them. But there is a difference in knowing someone versus offering genuine friendship, serving alongside one another, and studying our Bibles together.

Was I trying intentionally to exclude women with disabilities? Absolutely not. Was I trying to be unavailable and unhelpful to the parents who had children with exceptional needs? Of course not! But did I know *how* to engage those families, women, and children in a way that offered love, compassion, and a place of genuine belonging within the body of Christ? The answer was no. I had yet to experience life within the body of Christ from the fringes.

I naively thought all women would move from the fringe into the heart of the church—if they just put forth the effort. It was only through the birth of our first child who was later diagnosed with autism, that I really began to understand that one's own effort to move into the heart of the church and stay there was not something that I could control and solve by effort or desire. Life on the fringes of church was good for my heart. It taught me that it was not my lack of dedication to the church. It was not a lack of love offered by our congregation, and there was not a gap in my theology. The realities are that disabilities change the family and the family's ability to navigate church . . . for a lifetime.

Where my theology and practice failed me so many years ago was in thinking that my world was vastly different from other families who were touched by disability. Truthfully, I believe this is where many women and women's ministries are today—we do not realize the impact that the fall in Genesis chapter three has had on *all* of us—those who are neurotypical and those who are uniquely-abled. Each of us, as a result of the fall, has experienced a measure of brokenness in our bodies. Not only do our bodies wear out and break, not only do we experience the effects of sickness and death, but our intellectual, spiritual, social, and emotional capacities have all been marred by the fall. None of us are, this side of heaven, what we were designed to be—we are far from perfect.

Disability is simply a more visible form of brokenness.[1] Most adults have acquired sophisticated skills over the course of life, that have resulted in us being able to hide our weaknesses. Children, teens, and adults with disabilities cannot hide their brokenness. Their brokenness is on display for others to notice. Yet sin has affected every part of who we are—those with disabilities and those without. We are not as we were meant to be. Embracing our similarities, embracing the very core of our theology that recognizes the effect and the extent of sin on man and woman, changes the conversation about disability in women's ministry. It's no longer "us" and "the families touched by disabilities." Instead, it's just "us"—all of us, with all of our gifts and weaknesses working together to love and serve within the body of Christ until we are called home to heaven.

EMBRACING ONE BODY

It is easy and natural to surround ourselves with those who are like us. Our friends often share the same interests we have or have a similar perspective on life. With one click of a button, we can shape our social media feeds to reveal updates from the people we want to hear from and the perspectives that most encourage us. There is comfort and security in the familiar.

However, in Scripture, we find that the Kingdom of God embraces a different path. In 1 Corinthians 12, the apostle Paul describes what the body of Christ looks like: "the body is a unit, though it is made up of many parts" (1 Cor. 12:12). He goes on to elaborate on the nature of the different parts of the body: "If the whole body were an eye, where would the sense of hearing be? If the whole body were an ear, where would the sense of smell be?" (1 Cor. 12:17).

Why do we need the gospel to break into relationships within the body of Christ? Because left to ourselves we would prefer that the body of Christ look much more like we do than different. Using Paul's language of the human body, it makes perfect sense why diversity is needed in the body of Christ— without an ear, we cannot hear; without an eye, we cannot not see. If everyone were a leg, we would be effective at going places, but we would lack the ability to communicate, the ability to see where we were going, and the ability to hear those around us.

As we encounter real-life men, women, and children within the hallways of our church, our interactions are the practical basis on which our true theology is revealed. If conversation is easy and encouraging with someone, we might be inclined to seek them out again or invite that family over for a meal. If our initial interaction with visitors at church is awkward or strained, we might walk away pondering what went wrong, why it was awkward, and likely we will allow those feelings of discomfort to keep us from getting to know them. These responses to

initial interactions are not pre-contrived, yet we easily forget
1 Corinthians 12 to remember Paul's exhortation that we need
different parts of the body to make the church complete. Most
Christians do not intentionally exclude others who are different
than us—it's just easier to gravitate towards those who are
similar to us.

How is your women's ministry practically reflecting the
diversity in the body of Christ? Do you look around and notice
that there are many eyes but not ears? When you look around
a room filled with women who have gathered for Bible study,
are there women present from other races, different cultures,
various economic backgrounds, various educational levels, and
women who have disabilities both visible and invisible?

EMBRACING WEAKNESS

We probably do not often stop to consider what skills are
required to be an active participant in church. You have to be
able to get to church. You have to have social skills that allow
you to form friendships, carry on a conversation, or navigate
transitions within a worship service. You need reading skills to
read the order of worship from the church bulletin and in order
to sing the hymns. You need memorization skills to recite the
creeds and sing hymns from memory. It's also likely that you
need intellectual skills in order to understand the preaching and
teaching in your church so that you can grow in Christ.

Things that we do instinctively and skills that we take for
granted and use within the church are often significantly more
challenging and are barriers to women with disabilities. These
barriers prevent them from being able to fully participate in
the life of the church. Sometimes we may not intuitively know
that those needed skills are missing because of a disability.
And sometimes, because we do not know what *to do*, we end
up doing what we should not: ignoring those parts of the body
that are different than ourselves until they slowly slip to the
fringes of church and then eventually stop coming altogether.
Our actions reveal our true theology, which is why we need
Scripture to continually direct our path. First Corinthians 12:21-
22 says: "The eye cannot say to the hand, 'I don't need you!'
And the head cannot say to the feet, 'I don't need you!' On the

contrary, those parts of the body that seem to be weaker are indispensable, and the parts that we think are less honorable we treat with special honor."

When we read Scripture, there is a tendency on our part to assume the best possible motive and purity of action in applying it to our lives. If you read the passage above and thought, "I would never tell someone 'I don't need you,'" have you sought out and helped the elderly woman who lacks the fine motor skills to partake communion? Have you sought out the family that spends more time outside the church than inside the church due to a child's behavior problems? Have you noticed those who sit alone in the pews at church and gone out of your way to befriend them? Have you knelt down on the same level as a child with a disability or an adult in a wheelchair and told them how glad you are to see them today? Have you taken notice of those who do not make eye contact in the hallway and sought to encourage them?

Paul's words in 1 Corinthians 12:22 remind us that the seemingly weaker members of the body of Christ are actually the *indispensable* members. If we consider ourselves capable, able, and strong, this passage tells us what we likely do not want to hear—that we are not the indispensable part of the body of Christ that Paul is talking about here. Weaker members, whether they are babies or elderly, whether they have cognitive delays or have social deficits, whether they cannot stand or cannot speak—these members of the body of Christ are essential to the church order for it to function properly. They are indispensable. The body of Christ without its weaker members who have disabilities is still the body of Christ—but it operates at a deficit without them. Are we willing to change our view of "indispensable" from those members who are always ready and able to serve, to instead viewing the adult woman with cognitive impairment as the indispensable part of the body of Christ?

EMBRACING PEOPLE OVER PROGRAMS

The next logical question to ask is: "What do we do?" How *do* we modify our women's ministry in order to enfold women with disabilities? How *do* I overcome my fears of entering into the lives of other people who have very different daily lives than I do?

You do not need to worry about how much or little knowledge you have about disabilities. The world of disability is vast and ever-changing. Furthermore, what is true of one family with a disability might not be true for the next family. It is very easy to allow a fear of what we do not know or a fear of doing the wrong thing to unknowingly influence our relationships with women who have disabilities.

The first step towards embracing women with disabilities and their families is to take a relational step forward. Relationships always trump programs. It matters much more how you love, how you relate, and the effort you extend to develop that friendship than it matters "what you do." Yes, we want our friends with disabilities growing in their knowledge of God and His Word, but that learning always occurs in the context of relationships. Adaptations and accommodations are necessary, but when they are present in the absence of relationships, those adaptations and accommodations do not accomplish their true purpose of helping to enfold people with disabilities into the life of the church.

We often default to a program-driven approach to discipleship because it allows us to organize people and utilize resources. Do not create yet another set of programs for the women in your church with disabilities. To experience the blessings and benefits of church life, we need the women with disabilities to participate in the existing programs. We need to rub shoulders with the women with disabilities and serve together, study the Bible together, pray together, and share meals together. We need to learn and practice being present in someone's life without having an agenda. We need to practice the art of slowing down so we can learn from the women who are uniquely gifted.

How can your women's ministry adapt its existing women's ministry programs, Bible studies, and service opportunities to enfold *all* the women that God has in your church? Pray for eyes to see the women who used to be in the heart of the church and are now on the fringes due to the effects of aging. Pray for wisdom to know how to come alongside the wife who now has dementia and may disappear from church-body life due to outbursts or wandering. Pray for perseverance that you will become more comfortable with being uncomfortable. Pray for grace to go slowly since you cannot fix disabilities no matter how much you try to organize ministry.

Perhaps a next step could be a reverse-inclusion Bible study for a few young adults with disabilities in your congregation. Ask a small group of women to join these young adults for Bible study that is designed to meet unique needs. This allows you more flexibility of length of time, content taught, and maximizes fellowship and learning around the table for all.

The way to begin the conversation between women's ministry and disability ministry is not complicated nor do you need a special ministry team. At the heart of what is needed is compassion, willingness, and the desire to try. The heart of the gospel is that Jesus willingly came to earth to enter into and redeem the effects of sin and brokenness. We display Christ's love in the hallways each Sunday as we intentionally build and strengthen that relationship. We share in Christ's sacrificial love for us as we enter into relationships which may not be able to reciprocate.

As relationships develop, you will begin to understand true needs and not just perceived needs. One small step makes a tremendous difference in the life of a woman with a disability. Small steps over years lead women's ministry further into the heart of disability ministry at a pace everyone can sustain and support. Speed and programs are not the goal. Knowing and loving women is the goal. Seeing women who have disabilities love God and grow in their understanding of who He is and what He has done for them is where women's ministry and disability ministry should meet. When we see growth in grace and fellowship happening amongst women of all abilities, we will know that women's ministry and disability ministry have become inseparably entwined.

Ashley Belknap has an MA in Theological Studies (Reformed Theological Seminary). She is Director of Engaging Disability with the Gospel, the denominational disability ministry for the Presbyterian Church in America (PCA).

DISCUSSION QUESTIONS

1. Embracing Similarities – Read Genesis 3. In what ways do each of us experience brokenness in the body (physically, mentally, spiritually, socially) as a result of the fall? How do these realities impact the way that we view and interact with others who have visible and invisible disabilities?

2. Embracing One Body – Read 1 Corinthians 12:12-27. Use your own words to explain Paul's theology of the body of Christ and its many members. Practically speaking, how does this theology challenge us as we interact with those around us who are different than we are (consider disabilities, race, cultures, and personalities)?

3. Embracing Weakness – Re-read 1 Corinthians 12:22. Use your own words to define "indispensable." Now consider, with honesty, which types of women within your women's ministry you consider the indispensable members. How do we start to change our perspective so that we embrace Paul's theology that the weaker members are the indispensable ones?

4. Embracing People over Programs – What fears do you have about enfolding women with disabilities into your women's ministry? Be honest. What are your fears about this? What is a small step that you and your women's ministry could take this month, towards a lady or a family touched by disability? For example, how can you adapt Sunday school so that those with intellectual barriers are not excluded from the adult Sunday school realm?

1   Steph Hubach, *Same Lake Different Boat* (New Jersey: P&R Publishing, 2006), 27-31.

Chapter 12

Understanding the Transgender Struggle and How to Minister to Those Who Struggle
Ellen Mary Dykas

L ana was twelve years old when her occasional feelings of "otherness" were confirmed in a public and embarrassing way. She was out shopping for clothes with her mom, who asked a store clerk where to find jeans. Looking at Lana quickly, the store clerk answered with a surprising and unintended gut-punching question.

"What size does he wear?"

He?! Ashamed, Lana slowly looked up at her mom to catch her response, who quickly blurted out a number, corresponding to Lana's size for Junior Girls.

Lana grew up in the 1970s and never heard of the terms *gender dysphoria,* or *cisgender, transgender* or the idea of *non-binary* gendered persons. She considered herself a tomboy: a girl who enjoyed things that were more culturally associated with boys. On a daily basis, it actually wasn't a big deal that her sisters and friends seemed more "normal" in their preference for "girly" things like dolls and dresses. Lana enjoyed sports, and sure, she fantasized sometimes about being a boy and felt most comfortable in "boyish" clothes, but never thought she was a boy.

There are girls today who resonate with the adolescent Lana. They don't feel like they fit in with other girls when it comes to personal preferences. Their thoughts, desires and dreams may lean them in the direction of feeling more like a boy. The radical gender revolution has changed the direction of this conversation, however, since Lana was a girl. Young girls are now encouraged to consider that perhaps they don't *just like* boyish things. Perhaps they *are a boy* trapped in a girl's body.

REFRAMING AND DEFINING THE GENDER DISCUSSION
Less than five years ago, women's ministry leaders might not have encountered gender identity as an issue that their church needed to address with theological truth. Girls like Lana need compassionate and patient teaching from Scripture about what it means to be female. They need help understanding how God helps us with confusing feelings, thoughts and self-perceptions when it comes to gender. God's word is true, practical and engaging at every level of our humanity, including gender discomfort and dysphoria.

Genesis 1-2 and Colossians 1:16-17 are two passages which confirm that God created us in His image with an intended design for His purposes. The Bible reveals God as the loving Creator and holy Lord over His creation, yet contemporary society rejects this truth. Our me-first world worships personal autonomy and an individual's right to self-identify and re-create herself to be whatever she feels is best.

The idea of sculpting one's sexual and gender identity into whatever image a person prefers has gained traction. Concepts once commonly accepted as fixed, such as the gender binary of male or female, are now promoted by our culture as being experienced on a spectrum. We each have the right, it's thought, to define ourselves based on our personal feelings and experiences, to interpret life based on individual preferences.

"The idea of sculpting one's identity means that each person decides which subset of their personal life experience matters the most, such as their body, sexual attractions, social causes, careers, ethnicity, and feelings of maleness or femaleness. Each person has the right to determine who they are based on what they perceive to be most significant to them *personally*."[1]

The Bible addresses identity and gender with a radically different approach. Scripture never hints that God wants us to redefine ourselves into an image of our own making. Rather, it teaches that we are created, identified, and loved by our

Creator for His purposes and glory. The redemptive story of Scripture reveals a compassionate Savior in Jesus Christ who rescues us from ourselves, offering forgiveness and a new identity as loved children of God.

The Redeemer heals broken hearts and transforms gender struggles. Before considering how He accomplishes this, a quick review of the vocabulary often used in the transgender discussion is helpful.

- **Gender identity** – refers to an individual's personal sense/perception of being male, masculine, female, feminine, or a combination of the two or not associating with the gender binary at all.
- **Gender dysphoria** – a painful and confusing experience of emotional and psychological distress due to a conflict between personal understanding of gender identity and one's biological sex (anatomy, genitalia). Chaz Bono, who transitioned from a female identity as Chastity Bono said it this way: "There's a gender in your brain and a gender in your body. For 99% of people, those things are in alignment. For transgender people, they're mismatched. That's all it is. It's not complicated, it's not neurosis. It's a mix-up. It's a birth defect, like a cleft palate."[2]
- **Transgenderism** – an umbrella term for identifying or expressing a gender identity that does not match one's genetic sex. Thus, a "trans man," like Chaz, is a person born female who identifies as male. There are as many ways to express a transgendered identity as there are trans-identified individuals.
- **Gender bending/fluidity** – the belief that there is no "set" binary of male and female fixed by our genetic sex. Rather, gender is fluid as people experience it on a spectrum between male and female, sometimes moving around on the spectrum. Those who hold to gender identity fluidity believe that gender can morph from day to day.
- **Intersex** – the condition in which a person is born with sex characteristics or anatomy that does not allow them to be identified clearly as male or female at birth. This is a *physical* condition, not *psychological* like gender dysphoria.

GENDER: GOD'S DESIGN AND SIN'S IMPACT

Scripture identifies two biological sexes. "God created man in his own image, in the image of God he created him; male and female he created them" (Gen. 1:27). This verse explains our core identity: God creates us, and that includes being male or female. Genesis 1:27 is rich with meaning for the gender conversation. The first assignments of biological sex were divinely commanded and commended and ordained by God as expressive of both human need and divine nature. Elsewhere in Scripture, we see God involved in every detail of our creation, and that includes our biological sex (Ps. 139:13-16).

God's Word makes it clear that gender is ultimately about Him, *not us!* God reveals Himself throughout Scripture in images of gender. He is as a loving father (Heb. 12:5-9) and a loving mother (Isa. 66:13). Jesus affirms that two distinct biological sexes are necessary for marriage (Mark 10:6-8), and through their complementarity provide a beautiful human reality that points to the way Christ relates to His people (Eph. 5:22-33). The household of faith is comprised of beloved children who relate to each other as sisters and brothers with one Father. In creating us as male or female, God has entrusted us with a powerful way to reveal Himself to the world.

Sin's impact. Man's fall into sin wrought devastation upon every aspect of creation (including gender) and destroyed our ability to experience God's good design as He intended. Words like "broken," "disordered," and "distorted," are used to describe what Genesis 3:1-7 declares as the normal human experience. "The Bible's insight that we are all both created and broken is vital for understanding not just transgender questions but every kind of human affliction—physical or psychological. We have all been profoundly impacted by the fall."[3]

From conception each aspect of our natural state is corrupted and influenced by sin (Ps. 51:5). Fallen creation reaches to our bodies, which experience sickness, disease, missing parts, aging and ultimately, death. Our minds and thinking abilities are disordered. We believe and trust in lies and declare it truth. Brains are broken by illness and various physiological disorders. Our emotional life is also corrupted. We feel and express emotions that spew out selfishness, violence, jealousy and malice, to name just a few!

The most significant impact of sin is on our hearts, the volitional center from which we worship, make decisions and are motivated. Luke 6:43-45 explains how our behavior issues forth from our hearts. Left to our natural, fallen state, our hearts easily create and worship idols, demanding to live life autonomously. Embracing a transgender identity (*this is who I am*) is the fruit of a sinful heart's choices, responses, worship, and beliefs.

We are much more alike than different because of the fall! The transgender struggling girl or woman may seem very different from you, but she really isn't. Her sinful heart (like yours) is responding to life in a fallen and disordered world. Her body has physical challenges and limits. Her mind and emotional world need the healing of Christ through the Spirit's presence within and the renewal of God's transforming truth. Her belief system will need gentle guidance in being conformed to Scripture's teaching regarding gender, pain, sin, hope and redemption.

GOSPEL HOPE: TRANSFORMATION FROM THE INSIDE OUT

Contemporary messages in the cultural gender discussion offer many promises for transformation. One says that if you change your outside (appearance, body type, genitalia, etc.), then all will be made right on the inside. This idea encourages hurting girls and women to believe they can be liberated to be their true selves by doing all they can to "be" male externally.

However, real transformation through Jesus Christ starts on the inside and works its way outward. It's impossible to understand this without a worldview anchored in God's good created design and the impact of sin.

[God] has delivered us from the domain of darkness and transferred us to the kingdom of his beloved Son, in whom we have redemption, the forgiveness of sins (Col. 1:13-14).

I appeal to you therefore, brothers, by the mercies of God, to present your bodies as a living sacrifice, holy and acceptable to God, which is your spiritual worship. Do not be conformed to this world, but be transformed by the renewal of your mind, that by testing you may discern what is the will of God, what is good and acceptable and perfect (Rom. 12:1-2).

Our "outside" isn't our biggest problem, and our "inside" does not contain our true selves that need to be set free. The gospel of Jesus Christ declares the opposite! Transformation begins at the heart level through forgiveness and a lifelong process of sanctification. Through Christ's indwelling presence and a renewed mind/thought-life, our beliefs and behaviors gradually change as they align with God's Word.

The gospel gives female gender strugglers everything they need for faith and obedience. The path will involve painful self-denial, but all Christians are called to this. Jesus lovingly explained that, "If anyone would come after me, let him deny himself and take up his cross and follow me. For whoever would save his life will lose it, but whoever loses his life for my sake will find it" (Matt. 16:24-25).

HOW TRANSFORMATION HAPPENS: DISCIPLESHIP PRINCIPLES FOR GENDER STRUGGLERS

Friends, family, disciplers, women's ministry and church leaders: START here! If you sincerely want to help someone struggling with gender issues, consider the following.

1. Pray for compassion. A realistic understanding of any gender struggle must include a compassionate awareness of the agony a person feels. When we view a struggler through the lens of Genesis 1-3, we see her living in a "world that is broken at its core, resembling God's original design, but increasingly showing deep cracks and fissures in how God's image bearers live and reflect his image."[4]

2. Ask God to help you comprehend her pain. Sexuality and gender struggles often intimidate believers to the point

that they feel inept to attempt helping someone. Second
Corinthians 1:3-4 says we don't need to have a similar
experience of sin struggle and pain in order to understand
and love someone: "Blessed be the God and Father of our Lord
Jesus Christ, the Father of mercies and God of all comfort, who
comforts us in all our affliction, so that we may be able to
comfort those who are in any affliction, with the comfort with
which we ourselves are comforted by God." God will help you
to build "redemptive bridges" from your experiences of being
comforted in affliction into her gender struggle.

3. Come alongside through patient listening and learning.
Before sharing advice or biblical truths, seek to know her
story regarding gender identity/confusion. If she identifies as
transgender, ask how she came to this conclusion. What has her
journey felt like? Is God connected to her gender story?

4. Offer help, if she expresses a desire to receive it. With
children who are minors, the helping and directing is different
from coming alongside an adult, whom I have in mind here.[5]
Is this woman teachable? Is she open to what the Bible has
to say about her life situation? If not, and you proceed to give
(what you perceive to be) helpful advice and clarifying Bible
verses, you may cause more damage and bruise (or break) this
relationship. A willingness to pray and remain lovingly engaged
with an unteachable person *is not* giving up or giving in.

But what if she is wanting help? Now what?

PRACTICAL DISCIPLESHIP TO HELP GENDER STRUGGLERS
Discipleship is a process of helping someone know and follow
Jesus through a lifestyle of obedience and love. Coming
alongside someone wrestling with gender identity issues
will involve aspects of discipleship that apply to anyone. Let's
consider several and make specific application to someone
struggling with gender.

1. Explain what it means to follow Jesus. Regardless of age,
gender, socio-economic status, race, etc., all Christians are to

align every aspect of their lives under the loving kingship of Jesus. This is what we are proclaiming (whether we realize it or not!) every time we refer to the "Lord." He is our Father and Master, and because we belong to Him as daughters and servants, He has the right to govern our lives.

Often, we zealously focus on a specific sin, eclipsing the bigger picture of how to be a disciple of Jesus! This is one of the reasons why it's so important to consider point #3 above. What *is* her understanding of the gospel? Without a relationship with Christ or a willingness to submit to His holy authority, your discipleship of a woman who struggles with gender issues will not go very far. Refusing God's help or truth regarding gender is like the clay rejecting what the potter has crafted (Isa. 64:8).

Following Jesus means gradually acknowledging our need for God in every aspect of life, including our experience of gender. "Bringing God into the heart of the situation can do two things: it legitimizes the person's real distress with their inability to align their physical and psychological selves, and also injects another not-to-be-ignored dynamic: that the person's distress has an additional element of struggle to it, that to go against God's design and purpose does bring about increasing confusion and pain."[6]

2. Unpack a biblical view of identity.[7] "Gender struggle is often more than this, but it is never less than an attempt to satisfy the out of control desires of the heart. For gender strugglers, many of those desires are focused around the categories of identity and comfort."[8]

The idolatrous human heart craves autonomy. Embracing an unbiblical gender identity can feel comforting, even as it is an act of rebellion against God.

As a Christian wrestles with issues of gender identity, lead her to true identity: she is a loved, forgiven daughter of God and a female image-bearer. You'll need patience as those who find a "home" in a gender identity based on personal feelings usually are loyal and protective of it.

3. Guide her to turn towards God in faith and repentance.
Her journey will be unique, not a cookie-cutter, one-size-fits-

all. Here are several ways to help her walk forward in faith, building on the above points.

- Assist her in reading, praying and meditating upon God's Word.
- Help her recognize and flee temptation. She needs encouragement to avoid anything that entices her to turn from femaleness towards maleness or gender-fluid expressions. This might include social situations, entertainment, individuals who somehow "stir up" a desire to cover up her female identity. It also will mean a growing awareness of triggers, such as troubling emotions or circumstances that provoke a desire to seek comfort in trans-identifying behaviors (cross-dressing, speaking or acting in a way that is culturally male-conforming, etc.).
- Coach her to express her feminine self uniquely. Many women who struggle with gender issues feel confused, overwhelmed or insecure when it comes to "behaving and looking" like a woman. I guide women to do this in a way that is honoring to Christ (modest, not self-promoting), reflects their unique preference of style (jeans, skirts, collared shirts, flats, heels, jewelry *or not*, etc.) and is also generally accepted in their cultural surroundings as female conforming. Key to emphasize is that there is broad freedom in how each of us expresses ourselves as a female image-bearer; resist the urge to give a woman rules or guidelines that are extra-biblical!

4. Help her connect with spiritually vibrant community.
Living honestly and openly in relationships with others help us to experience and live out the gender that matches our biological sex. We need others to give us feedback on who we are and are to become. Rather than pushing for conformity to cultural gender stereotypes, help strugglers learn what godly relationships look like with both genders.

FINAL THOUGHTS FOR PARENTS OF YOUNG GIRLS[9]
Alongside the discipleship ideas above, here are a few added things to keep in mind for young children.

Model how to face discomfort and pain. Kids today grow up in a me-first world, with personal comfort ruling the day. Little girls who experience anxiety and internal turmoil need coaching on how to face it through Christ, rather than being "sheltered" by parents who make pain avoidance a priority. Facing trials in this life is to be expected; for some, a significant trial will be via gender struggles. Hebrews 4:16 invites God's people of all ages to come to Him for help and mercy whenever we need it. It's crucial for girls who experience gender dysphoria to learn how to collapse upon God's love and comfort instead of listening to answers the world gives.

Teach her about gender distinctions and avoid unbiblical stereotypes. Gender differences exist and they do matter. Stereotypes describe what is common to many girls or women, but they should never be "rules" for how we express our gender. Encourage girls to live in conformity with their birth sex of female without insisting on certain *cultural* expressions of gender as being biblical. Scripture gives latitude in how we express gender through our actions, and parents are to be on the front lines of modeling this to their kids.

Redirect a girl who expresses the desire to pursue medical action. We've already established that the deepest gender issues are internal. Gender confusion is not solved by puberty-blocking hormones or surgery, and often individuals who pursue this (with parental approval or as adults), often regret it later.[10]

If you are a sister in Christ struggling with gender dysphoria, your life is precious, and you are loved. Hear Jesus' promise: "I say to you, there is no one who has left the gender identity they felt more comfortable with, or the community they identified with, or the life they had expected and dreamed of, for the sake of the kingdom of God, who will not receive many times more—identity and community and life—in this time, and in the age to come eternal life."[11]

Ellen Mary Dykas is the women's ministry coordinator for
Harvest USA, a national ministry committed to discipleship
and church education on topic of sexuality, gender and
relationships. (www.harvestusa.org)

DISCUSSION QUESTIONS

1. If your experience with gender has not been difficult, what
   are ways your story of struggle and transformation might
   connect with women who do wrestle in this way? For
   example, do you ever attempt to "sculpt" an identity for
   yourself, rather than resting in Christ?

2. Review how the gospel brings hope for a girl or woman
   struggling with gender issues. Discuss the different ways
   your women's ministry can communicate these to a 12-year-
   old and a 32-year-old.

3. What obstacles are present in your church and women's
   ministry that hinder a spiritually vibrant community for
   gender strugglers?

4. What strengths are present to encourage them?

1   Ellen Mary Dykas, "The Unending Bending of Gender: Helpful or Harmful?" http://www.equip.
    org/article/unending-bending-gender-helpful-harmful/.
2   Quoted in Vaughan Roberts, *Transgender* (Purcellville, VA: The Good Book Company, 2016), 12.
3   Roberts. *Transgender*, 47.
4   Nicholas Black, "Gender Confusion: What do we say to someone?" *Harvest USA Magazine*, Fall
    2016, https://www.harvestusa.org/gender-confusion-what-do-we-say-to-someone.
5   See segment at the end of the chapter for specific ideas for helping young girls.
6   Black, "Gender Confusion."
7   Melissa Krueger, ed., *Identity Theft: Reclaiming the Truth of Our Identity in Christ* (Deerfield,
    IL: The Gospel Coalition, 2018).
8   Tim Geiger, *Redemptive Responses When Family Members Identify as Transgender*
    (Philadelphia, PA: Harvest USA, 2017), 4.
9   This section summarizes "Helping Parents Navigate the Gender Storm," a segment in "The
    Unending Bending of Gender: Helpful or Harmful?"
10 Jamie Dean, "Suffer the Children," https://world.wng.org/2017/03/suffer_the_children
11 Andrew T. Walker, *God and the Transgender Debate: What Does the Bible Actually Say About
    Gender Identity?* (Purcellville, VA: The Good Book Company, 2017), 119.

Chapter 13

Becoming an Encourager: How to Walk Beside Your Sisters in Christ
Christina Fox

Women's ministry is inherently relational. It's not a distant, hands-off kind of endeavor. It involves real people with real lives and real troubles. Those who serve women in their church need to be prepared to enter the lives of the women to know them and to walk alongside them as they grow in their faith.

One of the key elements of any relationship is encouragement. Scripture calls us to encourage one another (1 Thess. 5:11). Yet biblical encouragement is different than the encouragement we might hear voiced in the world. It's less about giving an inspiring message like a coach would give before the big game. It's more than boosting someone's self-confidence by saying, "You've got this!" It's also not saying what someone wants to hear—as though flattery can help someone endure suffering. Biblical encouragement goes deeper and speaks to the very heart and soul of another.

PARAKALEO AND BIBLICAL ENCOURAGEMENT
In the New Testament, the word used for "encourage" is *parakaleo*. This word means to call near, to invite or invoke.[1] It is used to call someone to one's aid and usually in the context of exhortation, encouragement, comfort, and consolation. *Parakaleo* is used in passages such as, "For you know how, like a father with his children, we exhorted each one of you and encouraged you and charged you to walk in a manner worthy of God" (1 Thess. 2:11-12); "But exhort one another every day, as long as it is called 'today,' that none of you may be hardened by the deceitfulness of sin" (Heb. 3:13); and "But

God, who comforts the downcast, comforted us by the coming of Titus" (2 Cor. 7:6).

The apostle Paul wrote the Corinthian church a letter admonishing them for problems plaguing the church, including issues with sexual immorality, conflicts between church members, and theological confusion about marriage, worship, and their engagement with pagan religion. First Corinthians is a stern letter, exhorting the church to turn from immorality and to grow in Christ-likeness. Paul sent Titus to deliver the letter and was anxious about their response.

After Titus returned, Paul wrote them another letter, 2 Corinthians. Titus had returned from his visit with the Corinthians with good news: the church had responded in repentance to Paul's previous letter. This brought Paul great joy. In 2 Corinthians, Paul wrote a letter in response to their repentance. He also used this letter to help them apply the gospel to specific situations they were going through, including suffering. Other than the book of Acts, 2 Corinthians uses the word *parakaleo* more than any other New Testament book.

Let's look at a passage from 2 Corinthians 1:

...the Father of mercies and God of all comfort, who comforts us in all our affliction, so that we may be able to comfort those who are in any affliction, with the comfort with which we ourselves are comforted by God. For as we share abundantly in Christ's sufferings, so through Christ we share abundantly in comfort too. If we are afflicted, it is for your comfort and salvation; and if we are comforted, it is for your comfort, which you experience when you patiently endure the same sufferings that we suffer. Our hope for you is unshaken, for we know that as you share in our sufferings, you will also share in our comfort (2 Cor. 1:3-7).

Paul had endured suffering, as had the Corinthian church. He revealed how difficult those sufferings were, "We were so utterly burdened beyond our strength that we despaired of life itself" (2 Cor. 1:8). He shared with them the comfort God gave him and used it to show how the gospel works in and through our sufferings. There are three lessons we learn from Paul in 2

Corinthians about what biblical encouragement looks like and how we extend it to the women we serve in ministry.

THREE LESSONS FROM 2 CORINTHIANS ON ENCOURAGEMENT

First, encouragement is grounded in our union with Christ. Verse five references our union with Christ, "For as we share abundantly in Christ's sufferings, so through Christ we share abundantly in comfort too." When Jesus came to earth and took on human flesh, He united Himself to us in our humanity. Through faith in His perfect life, sacrificial death, and resurrection from the grave, we are united to Him. His perfect life is credited to us. His death on the cross for our sins is credited to us. All the benefits of our salvation hinge upon our union with Christ. Because we are united to Him, we also share in His sufferings (see also Phil. 3:10-11). In our union with Him, we also share in comfort.

In this passage, Paul mentions how both his afflictions and comfort are shared with the Corinthians. In our union with Christ, we are also united to other believers. All who trust in Christ for their salvation are children of God. We are adopted into God's family and are brothers and sisters in Christ. Elsewhere, Paul compares the church to that of a human body with Christ as the head and we as the parts of the body. Just like a human body, when one part is injured, the rest of the body feels the impact of that injury. Likewise, when one part of our church body hurts, we all hurt. We all feel the pain of one another's losses and sufferings. "If one member suffers, all suffer together; if one member is honored, all rejoice together. Now you are the body of Christ and individually members of it" (1 Cor. 12:26-27).

Biblical encouragement is grounded in this union with Christ and one another. We are united to Christ in His sufferings and in His comfort as well as with other believers in theirs. When fellow believers hurt, we hurt. Not only do we share in the same sufferings, we also share in the same comfort (2 Cor. 1:6-7). We comfort one another out of the comfort and encouragement we've received from our union with Christ.

In our ministry to women in the church, we need to remember our union with one another. This knowledge ought to spur us on to comfort women with the comfort we've received in Christ.

Second, encouragement is spiritual. This passage teaches us that encouragement originates in God; He is the God of all comfort (2 Cor. 1:3-4). He is the source and wellspring. He comforts us, and then out of the overflow of that comfort, we comfort others. This means that our encouragement doesn't come from things or circumstances. It doesn't come from within us and our own abilities. While hearing words like "You've got this!" is inspiring, it doesn't enable us to achieve anything. Biblical encouragement points to resources and strength found *outside* ourselves and *in* Christ.

Biblical encouragement speaks to the soul of another believer. Through our union with Christ, we have the same Holy Spirit living inside us. When we encourage one another, we encourage one another through the Holy Spirit—the One whom Christ sent as the Comforter. Another name for the Holy Spirit is *paraklete* or "helper/counselor." "But the Helper, the Holy Spirit, whom the Father will send in my name, he will teach you all things and bring to your remembrance all that I have said to you" (John 14:26). The Holy Spirit does what *parakaleo* refers to because He comes to our aid.

When we encourage one another with the truth of who Christ is and what He has done, we are speaking to another's soul. We speak encouragement by speaking the gospel to our sisters. When a sister is battling sin, we need to remind her of her great need for Christ and how He fulfilled that need in His perfect life and sacrificial death. We remind her of the way of repentance and offer to walk alongside her in it. When a sister is in sorrow over the loss of a loved one or has just learned she cannot bear children or has received a terminal diagnosis, we weep with her. We remind her of the Man of Sorrows who endured the greatest suffering in our place. We remind our sisters that the Holy Spirit is always at work, even when they don't feel it, and will complete His work in making them like Christ. We remind them that nothing and no one can separate them from their Savior's love.

This passage also reminds us that God expects we *will* share our comfort with others. As it says in verse four, " . . . who comforts us in all our affliction, *so that* we may be able to comfort those who are in any affliction, with the comfort with which we ourselves are comforted by God" (emphasis mine). The encouragement God gives us in our sufferings is not for us to keep to ourselves; we must share it with others. Because we are united in Christ, such comfort does not belong to us alone—it belongs to the whole body of Christ. The comforts we receive are a testimony of God's grace, and we need to tell others about it, for their joy and encouragement.

As we minister to women in our church, we must point them to Christ and His work in them.

Third, encouragement includes loving correction. The word *parakaleo* also includes urging another person forward. It involves exhortation and correction. In his first letter to the Corinthians, Paul admonished them. They were influenced by false teachers and the culture in which they lived. They responded to his correction with repentance. When Titus came to visit the church, he learned of their repentance and it encouraged him, "Therefore we are comforted. And besides our own comfort, we rejoiced still more at the joy of Titus, because his spirit has been refreshed by you all" (2 Cor. 7:13). Titus returned to Paul to share their response with him, and Paul was also encouraged. In Paul's work with the Corinthian church, the gospel had come full circle, encouraging all involved.

Sometimes receiving such exhortation doesn't feel encouraging. It might even hurt, but a fellow believer who gently points out sin in another's life does so out of love. We are often blinded by our sin and need someone else to point it out to us. A Christian who lovingly points out our sin sees that we have wandered from Christ's will and call for our lives and wants to rescue us from harm. The Psalmist wrote, "Let a righteous man strike me—it is a kindness; let him rebuke me—it is oil for my head; let my head not refuse it" (141:5).

Such exhortation is not an opportunity for one person to point a finger at others. It's not about feeling superior by pointing out the faults of another. Rather, it is a believer who is grieved by another's sin pattern. Because we are united to one another, it hurts the body of Christ when believers turn away from living according to Scripture to do their own thing. Exhortation is always done out of love and gentleness. We go out of our way to speak to our wandering sisters in kindness, seeking to spur them on in the faith. As the apostle Paul wrote to the Galatians, "Brothers, if anyone is caught in any transgression, you who are spiritual should restore him in a spirit of gentleness" (6:1).

There are times the women in our church will need correction and exhortation. Perhaps as women share their lives with us during Bible study discussion, small group meetings, or in mentoring, we identify a sin pattern in their lives. It may be gossip or idolatry or bitterness toward someone else. Maybe it's a deeply rooted sin they have kept hidden for years. Whatever the sin, when we realize there is a sin issue that needs addressing, we should first pray for wisdom and discernment. We should then talk to the person privately, in truth and love. We should pray with and for her and offer to journey with her as she pursues repentance. We should also teach the women in our church how to give *and* how to receive exhortation.

As sisters in Christ, united by the blood of our Savior, our conversations with those we serve need to go deeper than motivational or flattering statements and to their very heart and soul. We must comfort, encourage, exhort, and urge them on in the faith, reminding them of who Christ is and what He has done.

Christina Fox serves on the Presbyterian Church in America's (PCA) national women's ministry team, is the editor of the *enCourage* blog, and is the author of *A Heart Set Free, Closer Than a Sister,* and *Idols of a Mother's Heart.*

DISCUSSION QUESTIONS

1. Who is the woman in your church that needs encouragement? Consider practical ways you can reach out to her: bring a meal, invite her to coffee, or write her a note. Use that outreach to offer spiritual encouragement.

2. What are some ways you can help the women in your church to encourage each other?

3. What are some ways you can make encouragement a vital component of your women's ministry? Consider taking the time each semester to meet with women individually and pray with them.

4. What are ways for your women's ministry to intentionally connect women who have experienced particular hardships with other women in similar trials to provide encouragement? (For example: Connect an older woman who has experienced a miscarriage with a younger woman who lost her baby.)

5. How can your women's ministry leadership team ask women to share their testimonies of God's comfort in their lives?

---

1   Strong, James. *Strongs Greek Dictionary of the New Testament* (Nashville: Thomas Nelson, 2001), 190.

Chapter 14

Help Her: Developing a Church-Wide Response for Vulnerable Women[1]
Ann Maree Goudzwaard

The following is a hypothetical story. The circumstances are derived from a variety of real and fictional situations. Some of the information in this chapter may trigger intense emotional responses. While I want to articulate biblical truth carefully on this topic, what can be conveyed in one chapter on this subject is limited. Please take this constraint into consideration.

Kelly felt like a little girl sitting in the oversized conference chair. The massive arms of the stately rocker seemed to swallow up all 110 pounds of her small frame. The chair was as intimidating as the five church elders seated across the conference table. Kelly's husband Rick sat next to her. Rick was an attractive guy with an average build. He was good-natured, smart, and loved by everyone in their small church. He worked with the youth group and tirelessly volunteered for almost every church event. Rick was also known for his vast knowledge of Scripture and theology. He was the envy of many wives who wished that their husband was half as godly. However, the person everyone else saw wasn't the man Kelly knew at home.

Every minute, an average of twenty people experience intimate-partner physical violence. "This equates to more than 10 million abuse victims annually."[2] Therefore, millions of women live in fear every day. In October of 2017, actress Alyssa Milano encouraged her Twitter followers to use the hashtag #MeToo if they had suffered from sexual harassment, sexual assault, or from an abusive relationship. The response was overwhelming, and #MeToo went viral. The #MeToo movement rapidly extended from the Hollywood "director's couch" to the front row of the church. Christian women began tweeting #ChurchToo. God's people soon discovered that religious communities are not immune to abuse.

Many women in the church have found comfort in sharing their stories. The #MeToo movement was a catalyst for creating a refuge on the Internet. Yet, the medium God ordained to rescue the weak and needy is not a little screen. The body of Christ is the entity, not technology. The church is called to pursue purity and peace and to glorify God (Heb. 12:14; 2 Peter 3:14). When men abuse their power and control in the home, Christ's body is blemished. Recent fall-out from scandals that cross denominational lines and other Christian traditions indicates that churches often fail to adequately address these horrific incidents. Yet Scripture tells us to relentlessly break up this fallow ground (Hos. 10:12). It is essential that men and women in church leadership adequately prepare to respond swiftly and compassionately to the cry of oppression.

It took everything within Kelly to approach her pastor and ask for this meeting. Normally, she would be silent. Kelly was skilled at hiding what went on behind closed doors, but the last time Rick threw her books against the wall, it pushed her over the edge. The book nearly hit their 4-year-old daughter in the head. Kelly felt she must do something to control Rick's outbursts.

THE WEB OF OPPRESSION

First, to articulate a biblical response to an abuse of power and control in the home, a biblically informed interpretive grid must be developed. Scripture is not silent on the topic of abuse. God hates all types of evil.[3] However, "abuse" can be an ambiguous term frequently directed toward a wide variety of situations in our culture. As we come alongside women who suffer from events outside their control, we want to be precise in our language in order to describe behavior that creates a climate of fear. The word "oppression" more accurately defines abuse from a biblical perspective.

Oppression is defined as an unjust or excessive exercise of power, or a corrupt exercise of authority, that causes a person harm. Scripture uses the term "oppression" almost fifty times in order to convey the crushing of an individual that creates a climate of fear.[4] Oppression is a misuse of power that finds expression in abuse.

Oppression includes physical force that is either direct physical contact or a demonstration of power that threatens bodily harm. It includes throwing things, damaging property, blocking a person's path/exit, raising a hand as if to strike, grabbing, pinching, etc.

Oppression also encompasses what might be referred to as emotional or psychological abuse. In Psalm 55, the psalmist has not experienced any physical harm, but what he suffers is considered oppression. There is a misuse of power that results in shame and humiliation (Ps. 55:1-3, 12-13; Prov. 12:18a). This oppression manifests itself in the form of unrelenting criticism, verbal threats, belittling, isolation, or manipulation.

Oppression can be used by one person against another in demanding exacting amounts of money or withholding support (1 Tim. 5:8; Matt. 18:27-30.) In oppressive relationships, a domineering partner might keep financial information hidden from the other partner in order to exert control over their freedom or spending habits.

Oppression might use a woman's faith in order to control her behavior. Those who use spiritual means to dominate have been known to force their partners to extreme disciplines (Ezek. 34:20-22). These may include (but not be limited to) making the woman practice prolonged periods of prayer, extensive Bible reading, or unnecessary fasting. She may not be allowed to attend church, or only be permitted to do so at the discretion of the oppressor.

Oppression may use sex as a form of abusive power. In fact, this is one of the most difficult forms to detect. It includes any of the ways a perpetrator might use it in order to achieve sexual stimulation against a woman's will. He may force her into intercourse or to perform certain sexual acts or to view pornographic materials against her will.

Kelly knew that if she told the elders that Rick was throwing books at her, they would think he simply had an anger problem. She contemplated the consequences should she elaborate on what would transpire after a "book throwing" event. They had been arguing the first time Rick picked up her Bible and devotional and threw them across the room. Rick thought she spent too much time reading and not enough time planning and fixing meals, doing laundry, or cleaning the house. Kelly worked hard to keep their house neat and orderly, and she enjoyed cooking. It seemed like whatever she did, it was never enough for Rick. When he came home from work, he was always critical of her. He'd tell her she was good for absolutely nothing and mock her by asking, "An excellent wife, who can find?" Kelly chalked it up to stress at work. The second time Rick threw her books, he actually threw them at her. He had come home from work that night visibly agitated. He picked up her phone, checked her text messages (which he did every night), and saw—what he thought—were far too many texts from her mom. Kelly didn't know what hit her until she saw her Bible on the floor next to her feet. It hit her lip, but didn't leave a bruise. However, what happened in their bedroom that night when Rick wanted to "make up" (his words) definitely caused significantly more pain and damage.

HARD-HEARTED

One of the leading experts in this field of study suggests that the profile of an "abuser" varies considerably.[5] One day he might be loving and attentive, while the next he is violent and out of control. *Why does he do that?* is the question that author Lundy Bancroft tries to answer in his book of the same name. He suggests that men who oppress feel a sense of entitlement and are justified in their actions. I appreciate Bancroft, and others like him, who have substantial experience counseling oppressors. They are incredibly helpful to the church for identifying and calling out the destructive behaviors of oppression. However, in this chapter I want to take their work one step further and ask Scripture why men act this way. For the church to address this behavior biblically, we need to identify the heart issues of oppressors.

God's original design for oneness led to a gentle subjection between men and women (Gen. 1:28).[6] The fall distorted this design, and a sinful desire to control in anger ensued (Gen. 3:16; 4:8; Judg. 19; Ps. 82:3-4; James 4:1-3). Behind the abuse of power and control by men in the home are sinful thoughts, emotions, and actions. These are not men with a mind for Christ. At the core of this issue is the fact that the oppressor has lost sight of his love and faithfulness to God. It is from within this void that his evil actions find life. Because oppressive behavior is a heart issue, it is important for our discussion to note what it is *not*.

Oppressive behavior in the home is not a marital problem.
No matter what a woman does or does not do, she is not responsible for her husband's sinful behavior. Women may respond unbiblically to a husband's sin, and these responses should be attended to in the process of caring for this family. However, the primary concern is to secure the woman's safety, and then help the man reconcile his violent heart toward God.

Oppressive behavior in the home is not merely an anger problem.
"For with hearts like an oven they approach their intrigue; all night their anger smolders; in the morning it blazes like a flaming fire" (Hos. 7:6). Hearts, similar to an oven smoldering, are an undetected fervor until a suitable opportunity arises. Wickedness within is fed and nourished until the heart breaks forth angrily when the occasion seems fitting. Anger is certainly one of the tools used to intimidate and control. However, the heart of the issue is the man's sinful desires that war within him (James 4:1-3).

Oppressive behavior in the home is not provoked by the wife.
In 1 Samuel 8, God provides us with the characteristics of a person that "rules"oppressively over those in his care.

"These will be the ways of the king who will reign over you: **he will take** *your sons and appoint them to his chariots and to be his horsemen and to run before his chariots. And* **he will appoint for himself** *commanders of thousands and commanders of fifties, and some to plow his ground and to reap his harvest, and to make his implements of war and the equipment of his chariots.* **He will take** *your daughters to be perfumers and cooks and bakers.* **He will take** *the best of your fields and vineyards and olive orchards and give them to his servants.* **He will take** *the tenth of your grain and of your vineyards and give it to his officers and to his servants.* **He will take** *your male servants and female servants and the best of your young men and your donkeys, and put them to his work.* **He will take** *the tenth of your flocks, and you shall be his slaves. And in that day, you will cry out because of your king..." (1 Sam. 8:11-18, emphasis mine).*

Oppressive rulers are "takers." Conversely, just rulers who act lovingly toward others are "givers" (John 3:16). Paul tells us that a husband who loves his wife will sacrificially *give* himself up for her (Eph. 5:25).

The pattern of belittling, book-throwing and forced, physically violent sex continued throughout their marriage. Over time, Rick didn't even have to speak or act in order to let Kelly know what he was thinking. All he had to do was brush his hand on her books when he walked past the sofa table, and Kelly would understand she had better fall in line quickly. In fact, Rick made sure Kelly acted a certain way in public using the same technique. Kelly eventually learned to hate anything having to do with books.

Kelly looked at the church leaders. She could see it in their eyes—they weren't grasping the magnitude of what she endured in her home. Her veiled attempt at revealing only what was safe to reveal fell flat. Kelly sensed the tension in Rick's body as he explained away everything she had told them. At some point she heard him say thank you and how grateful he was that the elders had taken precious time to help him and Kelly work out what was really just a lover's spat. As they got ready to leave the meeting, all she could think about

was Rick's hand on the Bible in front of him and how he had
gently slid it over the table in her direction.

CITIES OF REFUGE
Often, women in violent homes find it difficult to reveal that
they need help. If they speak of the threat in their home, they
risk escalating the danger. This makes it difficult to draw
these frightened women out. Kelly's situation raises some
good questions for us to consider in order to create a refuge to
which an oppressed woman can run.

Should church leaders encourage a woman to escape to
safety? I am aware that this is controversial. Therefore, each
situation should be determined on a case-by-case basis. In the
situation when a child might be in potential risk of serious
injury, physical or emotional or sexual harm, and/or death,
the response is handled swiftly and decisively. When a woman
seeks safety from similar cruelty, the best course of action is
to act quickly to protect her; err on the side of her welfare.[7]

Are church leaders and women's ministry leaders
responding to sufferers wisely? Sometimes, women are silent
because of the responses they've heard in the past:

> "If she would just submit . . ."
> "If she would stop taking control in the home . . ."
> "If she would quit calling the shots . . ."
> "If she would study God's Word more . . ."
> "If she could just be patient with God . . ."

Certainly, a woman in this situation might benefit from
counsel. However, until the full story is uncovered, we need
to restrain from a careless application of Scripture to her
situation (Prov. 18:13).

Are leaders encouraging biblical submission? An
oppressive husband often has an unbiblical view of
submission that he has used to coercively control his wife.
It includes rigid, legalistic adherence to ideas that are not
substantiated biblically. The last thing a woman will want to
hear as her church comes alongside her is that she should
submit—to anyone, including her church leaders. It is

imperative that the woman comprehend *biblical* submission in order to learn to lean on the Father and His ordained (godly) authority. Biblical submission in marriage is "as to the Lord" (Eph. 5:22). These passages directly link the husband's authority over his wife with Christ's authority over the church. It is a "servant-authority, an authority with responsibility"[8] for those who are under a leader's care (Matt. 20:25-28). The pastors and elders of the church hold the keys to the kingdom (Matt. 16:19). By bringing the gospel to bear on the husband's heart issue of oppression, to urge him to admit his sin and recognize his need for a Savior, church leaders help protect the wife. We want to encourage her to trust in this process.

Are we extending grace? Giving grace means that we help a woman respond to her situation proportionately—balancing the truth she may need to hear with consolation. In 2 Corinthians 1, Paul tells us the characteristics of one who gives comfort: they are afflicted, they are sufferers, they have been comforted, and they have hope (vv. 4-7). It is from the hope in Christ that we found in our own despair that we minister to others in theirs. We are no better than those we serve—we simply walk one step ahead and reach back to gently guide them toward the hope we have found ourselves.

Are we pointing her back to the gospel? An oppressive husband may have used scriptural truth as a weapon for power. We may need to reintroduce these women to God's holy, trustworthy, and good Word. In our union with Christ, we reflect His power of grace to do good, to persevere in times of need, to say "no" to temptation, to communicate in love, and to live holy and godly lives. Colossians 1 tells us that, because of this hope, we are compelled to respond biblically to life's circumstances. Are we encouraging these women to place their hope in the power of the gospel?

Are we exhibiting humility? We don't have all the answers (2 Cor. 3:5). We can't explain God's intent. We know that He is sovereign and good, but we don't know why He has allowed sinful men to do sinful things (Deut. 29:29; Prov. 16:4; Luke 22:3; Rom. 8:28). Yet, we know HIM, and we can encourage a woman by what we know to be true about Him (Job 26:7-14a; Heb. 12:3).

HELP(H)ERS

Are church leaders utilizing the gifts of the entire church body? The church is uniquely qualified to meet an oppressed woman's needs very practically. This is accomplished most effectively by involving women at every stage of helping a woman in distress. For instance, one of the major reasons a woman stays with her oppressive husband is financial. Her concerns in leaving an oppressive relationship range anywhere from where to live to how to attend required appearances in court. Women in the church can come alongside and offer care for the children, arrange carpools, accompany the woman to scheduled court appearances, deliver meals, and, of course, pray with and for her.

What happened to "Kelly" in my fictitious story might not have ended as it did if a female advocate/helper had been in the room. Another woman sitting in on the conversation, listening with both her eyes and ears, might have picked up on subtle insinuations and language cues. She might have been able to take note of the changes in Kelly's body language and follow up with her after the meeting in an attempt to glean more information.

A woman who is a godly, mature Christian can be an advocate for women like Kelly. This advocate is not only an asset *for* the woman but also *to* her on behalf of the church leaders.[9] As a female advocate listens in on conversations between the woman and her leaders, she hears the same things the woman did and, after the meeting is over, she can help her to respond appropriately.

I chose this hypothetical story intentionally in order to highlight the difficulty women have in sharing intimate details with a group of men. It may not be appropriate for a woman to be quite so specific about sensitive information. Having another woman present may provide the support she needs to bring this information to light. Another woman in the room also serves the leaders as somewhat of a hedge of protection for their purity.

As the body of Christ, we must not ignore those who cry out to us for help. All the more so, we must run interference for those who are unable, of their own accord, to seek relief in their need. Scripture requires that the entire church respond biblically and compassionately to all forms of oppression. By developing a response to oppression at every level, the church can be a refuge to rescue the weak and needy. Through the compassionate caregiving of church leaders, the oppressed are surrounded in His love, the church's purity is preserved, and the name of the Lord is glorified.

Ann Maree Goudzwaard, MDiv (Reformed Theological Seminary) is a certified biblical counselor and the Director of Communications for the Institute for Biblical Counseling and Discipleship.

DISCUSSION QUESTIONS

1. What are some of the specific, unique gifts of the women in your area of ministry that can be utilized to help the weak and the needy?

2. What tangible steps can leaders in your church take to show that you can be trusted to advocate on their behalf?

3. What can leadership do to encourage women in the church that they can be trusted with sensitive information?

4. What are some practical ways Women's Ministry leaders can start helping the weak and needy?

5. Who can Women's Ministry leaders include in serving alongside in "one- another" care?

1 I am indebted to Chris Moles and his work on domestic violence in the home. *The Heart of Domestic Abuse: Gospel Solutions for Men Who Use Control and Violence in the Home* (Bemidji, MN: Focus Publishing, 2015).
2 Nationally. https://ncadv.org/statistics.
3 Much of the material used to develop this section is derived from a collaboration between myself and senior staff at Christ Covenant Church, Matthews, NC, in developing a plan for a church-wide response to domestic abuse. My contribution to the project included research. This section is loosely developed from a position paper written by Bernie Lawrence and Susan Shepherd. *Domestic Abuse: How a Church can Respond Biblically, Wisely, and Compassionately*, 2018. Copies upon request: info@christcovenant.org
4 Ibid.

5   Due to what I consider as this author's theological and biblical deficiencies, I would not
    recommend his book. However, Bancroft's years of experience merits our attention to his
    observations of the collective behavior of those who oppress. Lundy Bancroft, Protective
    Mothers Alliance International, *Abuser Profiles,* taken from *Why Does He Do That? Inside the
    Minds Of Angry and Controlling Men.* https://protectivemothersallianceinternational.org/
    category/abuse/

6   John Calvin, *Calvin's Commentaries (Complete),* trans. John King; Accordance electronic ed.
    (Edinburgh: Calvin Translation Society, 1847), paragraph 375. https://accordance.bible/link/
    read/Calvin#375

7   Dr. James Newheiser, (2017). *Helping Churches to do a Better Job Handling Cases of Abuse.*
    [online] Jim Newheiser. Available at: https://jnewheiser.ibcd.org/helping-churches-to-do-a-
    better-job-handling-cases-of-abuse/.

8   John Frame, *Systematic Theology; An Introduction to Christian Belief* (Phillipsburg, NJ: P&R
    Publishing, 2013), 796.

9   Christ Covenant Church, Matthews, NC "Shepherdess Packet for Interested Parties." Copies
    upon request: info@christcovenant.org

Chapter 15

Discipleship for Women in the Workplace

Jeany Kim Jun

This chapter is intended for both leaders in women's ministry ministering to women in the church who work and for women working outside the home. Leaders will gain a better understanding of women in the workplace in order to equip them to evangelize and disciple at work. For women who work, this chapter provides a framework for evangelism and discipleship in your chosen place of work.

Sometimes people may think that just going to church on Sundays is enough. But Jesus calls us to something bigger. He calls us to make disciples (Matt. 28:19). If you are a Christian, you are called to be a disciple-making disciple. Whether you are a stay-at-home mom or work full-time, you are called to work "as working for the Lord" (Col. 3:23). Don't worry. Jesus doesn't send you out alone, but says, ". . . I am with you always. . ." (Matt. 28:20). So then, how do you make disciples? You first need to *be* a disciple.

Gospel Foundations,[1] a Bible study book on discipleship, outlines five elements of discipleship. First, disciples *learn* from Jesus in the context of a relationship. Second, disciples *obey* Jesus without condition. Third, disciples are *called* by grace. Fourth, disciples are *sent* on a mission for the souls of men and women. Finally, disciples *treasure* Jesus above everything else.[2]

God placed each of us in a specific place whether it be a classroom, a clinic, or a kitchen. He providentially surrounded us with the people within our sphere that only we can encounter. It turns out that our spheres are not limited to our immediate church community. We have the opportunity to share the good news of Christ with the people God placed in our lives and present the message of hope by planting seeds and watering faith.

I have been a pharmacy professor and licensed pharmacist for the past seventeen years. My spheres of influence include my class of eighty students, rotation students, patients, and co-workers. I finally came to realize that God placed me where I am to bring the message of hope in Christ and to be the light to these diverse groups of people. I admit that I did not start out evangelizing and discipling people in the workplace. It took a while for me to learn how to be intentional and purposeful in my relationships and learn how to recognize open doors to usher Christ into my conversations.

When I first started working, I felt disconnected to my students because I had compartmentalized my spiritual life and my professional life. I thought I was only supposed to guide them to become competent clinicians and thus never touched upon the whole person, to love and serve others with the gifts and skills God gave them.

I memorized 1 Peter 3:15, "*Always be prepared to give an answer to everyone who asks you to give the reason for the hope that you have*" (NIV) but failed to utter my answer aloud when given the opportunity. During my first year teaching, I was assigned three students: a Muslim, a Buddhist, and a Jewish student. At the end of the rotation, I took them out to lunch. In the car, the Jewish student asked, "Dr. Jun, you seem to have a lot of peace. Where does that come from?"

Here it was, an opportunity to share my faith. In my heart, I was happy to have been asked this question and answered silently to myself, "It's because of Jesus." But other thoughts crept into my mind, "Wait, the other students are here, what would they think?" After a few seconds of silence, I couldn't say anything except, "Um, you know . . . it's just . . ." I was relieved that we arrived at our destination and got out of the car but knew I had squandered this perfect opportunity.

Throughout lunch I was reminded of this verse, "*Whoever is ashamed of me and of my words, of him will the Son of Man be ashamed . . .*" (Luke 9:26). I felt awful. I justified how inappropriate it was to share my faith at work. Then I realized, she asked me! If someone asks, then I am free to answer. Since then, God graciously provided other opportunities to communicate the gospel in the workplace. My whole work trajectory is a story of God's leading; hence, I openly share how we moved to Cambodia for three years, which naturally leads students to ask me why. This creates openings to reveal my faith in Christ.

In women's ministries, it seems that working women are a neglected group, and outreaches and ministry opportunities often overlook enfolding them. How can women's ministry leaders take seriously the ways in which they can equip the working women in their church to be more intentional and help cultivate a discipling culture for women in their workplaces?

Women's ministry leaders must first recognize that they are ministering to a diverse group of women who may be stay-at-home moms to full-time employees. In order to reach all groups, leaders can first encourage *all* women to be discipled within the church and be mindful of their work schedules. The message has to be clear that each woman, whether or not she works outside the home, is a precious child of God and that her identity is no longer as an orphan but is secure as a daughter of God. Next, leaders must understand that women who work have the world speaking into their lives, demands that are made at work, and at home. They may have a tremendous amount of guilt because they are working and not at home with the children. Our churches are a place where the message of her identity in Christ should ring louder and clearer than what the world says. The church needs to have a vision for women to disciple other women, both inside the church and out, even in the workplace. This vision needs to be articulated clearly and repeatedly and taught within a discipleship curriculum. As women in the church are discipled, they can learn the practical aspects of how to disciple others, facilitate small groups, and understand the nuances needed to talk about their faith in the workplace. Working women who spend 20-40 hours a week at work know what a significant amount of time it takes to build relationships with co-workers. Women's ministry leaders must lead by articulating the need to intentionally reach women to go beyond their church community. Although some may assume that discipleship is exclusively for believers who are already in the church, discipleship actually begins with evangelism. We see this example with Jesus who first called some unknowing fishermen to follow Him. Jesus called His disciples to be witnesses to the ends of the earth, so we, too, are called to make disciples in all our spheres of influence.

One way to carry out the Great Commission is *intentionality.* Like it or not, God placed you exactly where you are. Therefore, get to know the people around you. Meet them outside of the workplace. Working women must be willing to invest in the women in their workplaces, develop rapport to share their faith, and remind them of the hope in Christ. Author Susan Hunt says to invest in people rather than in programs or projects, to encourage and equip them to live for God's glory.[3]

Traeger and Gilbert, in *The Gospel at Work,* recommend to "develop mentoring relationships with one or more employees. Young workers are starving for career counseling and wisdom from older, more experienced Christians who can help see how the gospel should impact their work lives."[4]

For me, it meant taking students on medical mission trips to Cambodia. God showed me that I have an exciting purpose as a pharmacy professor. I have the privilege to inspire the next generation of Christian pharmacy students to live and work for God's kingdom. Therefore, I continuously invest intentionally in these relationships. One of these intentional relationships with a student blossomed into a mentoring relationship, both professionally and spiritually, when she joined my discipleship group.

Additionally, look for opportunities God creates for you. When you work in your job as for the Lord, work with excellence. You should demonstrate faithfulness and integrity (Col. 3:24) and work "without grumbling or disputing" (Phil. 2:14). The watching world sees how you navigate challenges, difficulties, and suffering. Christian witness is often most striking to others in and through our suffering and our response to it. Life in Jesus does not mean a life absent of suffering. In fact, it often means the opposite. "In this world you will have trouble," our Lord said in John 16:33. However, to suffer well means to acknowledge the words of Christ with the hope and promise of ultimate victory in Christ. "But take heart! I have overcome the world." In other words, to suffer well means to suffer with hope of eternal joy. This is what God's children do—suffer well as the rest of the world watches and marvels at what it means to be a follower of Christ.

Hence, don't be afraid to share your struggles with close colleagues. This vulnerability makes your faith more real rather than less attainable. As your relationships develop, people can witness how you progress through your trials and consider the "reason for the hope that you have" (1 Peter 3:15). Some people may desperately need to hear the specific words you have for them. It might not be the gospel, but it may be an encouragement to someone about to lose hope.

I have a colleague who was having a hard time in her marriage. Previously, I shared about my own difficulties with unforgiveness with a family member because my daughter was bitten on the face by their dog. As time went on, she shared her own struggles with her family. One day, she passed me a note that said, "I'm falling under the weight of my cross today, could you help me get back up? I'm feeling so hopeless today."

Not knowing exactly what to say, I shared what I learned from a sermon about Jacob and his dysfunctional family— how God redeemed the situation, using Leah, the unloved one, to bring about the line of Jesus. Astonishingly, she felt like God was using me to speak into her life as she had just read a blog about Leah. I also shared that when we focus on others' sin, we fail to see our own sin and reminded her that before God, we are all miserable sinners. She said, "You're right, I am such a big sinner. I couldn't see my sin in all this because I was focused on the other person's sin." She added, "Thank you for giving me hope today. You can be the greatest evangelist, but if you cannot give hope to someone, it's meaningless." It takes time to build trust. I worked with her for two years before I had this type of conversation at a time when she was in the midst of her family crisis. This encounter emboldened me to ask if she wanted to go through a discipleship book[5] with me. She said, "Of course! I need all the help I can get." People do not enter our lives by accident. Speaking truth in love allows others to listen, and we use the relational capital built over time to disciple them in a relational way. Remember, God put you where you are for His purposes to extend His kingdom.

Finally, learn to articulate the gospel effectively. I failed miserably in the past because I was not fluent in the gospel. In *The Great Debate* between Dr. Gordon Stein, a staunch atheist, and Dr. Greg Bahnsen, a Christian philosopher, Dr. Stein asked, "Is God good?" Dr. Bahnsen replied, "Yes, He is." Dr. Stein then asked, "How do you know that?" Dr. Bahnsen answered with a simple, yet clear, articulation of the gospel. He said, "He saved me. He created me. He made the world and he made it good. He sent his son into the world to die for my sins."[6] We can all learn how to do this. We don't need a theological degree to articulate our faith with non-believing colleagues. As we are overwhelmed by the irresistible love of Christ, we will be compelled to tell others about Him—even our co-workers.

Jeany Kim Jun is a pharmacy professor. She served in Cambodia for three years as a medical missionary, and currently serves as Director of Discipleship at New Life Presbyterian Church of Orange County.

DISCUSSION QUESTIONS

1. In what ways are you being intentional in your relationships and kingdom-minded in the workplace?

2. What opportunities have you had to share the gospel with your co-workers?

3. In what ways is your church being intentional about training women to disciple women in the workplace?

1   Albert Shim and Pacific Crossroads Church, *Gospel Foundations Leader's Guide* (Los Angeles, CA: Pacific Crossroads Church, 2010), 11.

2   Ibid.

3   Susan Hunt, *Spiritual Mothering* (Wheaton, IL: Crossway Books, 1992), 5.

4   Sebastian Traeger and Greg Gilbert, *The Gospel at Work* (Grand Rapids, MI: Zondervan, 2013), 122.

5   Bob Thune and Will Walker, *The Gospel-Centered Life*, World Harvest Mission (Greensboro, NC: New Growth Press, 2011).

6   Greg Bahnsen and Gordon Stein, *The Great Debate: Does God Exist?* (video). Available at: https://www.youtube.com/watch?v=anGAazNCfdY

Chapter 16

What Is Time Worth? Sabbath Principles for Rest for the iScreen Generation

Catherine Cook

The pressure to perform as women has never been higher. We often internalize messages that tell us our self-worth will be achieved when we can look at our lives and say, yes, we have succeeded at school, career, motherhood, in relationships, and in the fitness and appearance of our bodies. The problem with this calculation for worth is that it is ever-allusive. So, we keep working at it—working on ourselves, improving ourselves, focusing on *ourselves* because the waters of success and self-interest are deep and murky, with the false promise that something desirable lies beneath. These waters seem particularly enticing at the beginning of adulthood when choices young women make can shape the course of the rest of their lives—whether they *will* be successful in their career or relationships. This also makes these choices weighty and anxiety-inducing.

Between attending college and ministering to college-aged women, I have spent the last decade on the campuses of highly selective colleges, and I have noticed a trend in the last few years as Millennials have graduated to begin their careers and the new younger generation, Generation Z, has entered college. There has been a lot written in the last few years on this rising generation, especially on their attachment to technology, and they have been referred to as "screen teens" since they have never known a world without a smart phone. What many people miss when they focus on the increased consumption of social media is the opposite but equal trait of this new generation: discipline. It's true that young adults waste an inordinate amount of time watching cat videos, but they also are adept at utilizing their time and their time on the internet for optimal productivity, often accomplishing several things on their devices at one time, hoping to achieve a bright—and *stable*—future.[1]

It has always been true that in these competitive environments, students' days revolve around "keeping up" with their peers' apparent success. These competitive environments and the effort that students make to get into highly selective universities train them to view their own production as of higher worth than their person, or, for their person to be inseparable from their production. This is even more true of the newest generation that is known for their ability to think and produce at high quantities.

In addition to failing to honor our own inherited worth as image-bearers of God (Gen. 1:27), unhealthy self-improvement leads to unintentional selfishness. For young people in particular this selfishness sneaks up on them. It starts out as a way for them to honor their parents—to fulfill their parents' desires for them to do well in school and to utilize their gifts and opportunities. However, when self-improvement becomes the mantra a child learns growing up, it becomes harder and harder for that child to step back and self-evaluate their goals when they leave home and enter early adulthood. Consequently, as I have observed driven young women succeed, I have also observed them self-isolate. This is not usually done on purpose or even for selfish reasons, but rather because self-focus is what the self-improvement required while they were growing up.

When we minister to the young women of this generation, we need to remember that while the challenges of this new generation may be modern, they are not new. Like all good gifts, time has been consistently misused by mankind. What does Scripture say about the purpose of time as it relates to man in Scripture? Jesus responded to the misuse of time in Matthew 12 when the Pharisees twice confront Jesus on His lack of discipline in regard to the Sabbath. In His response, Jesus derives His authority from a source the Pharisees accept, the Scripture, and a source they reject, Himself.

The first time the Pharisees confront Jesus is when His disciples were hungry and picking grain on the Sabbath: "Look! Your disciples are doing what is not lawful to do on the Sabbath" (Matt. 12:2). Jesus responds to this accusation of Sabbath-breaking with two scriptural precedents. The first precedent from 1 Samuel 21:1-6 is the story of King David taking bread consecrated to God and set aside for the priests and feeding it to his hungry companions. The second precedent is that of the priests who had to perform their priestly duties on the Sabbath and thus "desecrate the Sabbath, yet they are innocent" (Matt. 12:5 NIV).

While the Pharisees recognize the importance of King David and the importance of priestly duty, they fail to affirm the importance of Jesus' own authority:

I tell you, something greater than the temple is here. And if you had known what this means, 'I desire mercy, and not sacrifice,' you would not have condemned the guiltless. For the Son of Man is lord of the Sabbath (Matt. 12:6-8).

Twenty centuries after the Pharisees rejected Jesus' teachings on the Sabbath, Rabbi Jacob Neusner, in his book *A Rabbi Talks with Jesus* explains why, if confronted with Jesus and His teachings in the 1st century, he would have argued against Jesus rather than joined ranks with His disciples. Rabbi Neusner argues that a faithful Jew must "enter a dissent at the teachings of Jesus, on the grounds that those teachings at important points contradict the Torah."[2] Therefore, rather than seeing Jesus as the Lord of the Sabbath, Neusner views Him as a Sabbath-breaker: "by criterion of the Torah, Israel's religion in the time of Jesus was authentic and faithful, not requiring reform or renewal . . ."[3] If Neusner is correct, this would mean Jesus' heart for mercy contradicts the authentic meaning of the law because it contradicts the letter of the law.

On the surface of things, it would appear that Neusner is right. After all, the fourth commandment spoken by God was to set apart the seventh day of the week on which the Lord Himself had rested from His work of creating: "On it you shall not do any work" (Ex. 20:10). It does not say, "You shall not do any work unless they are acts of mercy." It says, "You shall not do *any* work." Neusner's view is that "the Torah was and is perfect and beyond improvement."[4]

Evangelical Christians claim a similar doctrine of Scripture called "inerrancy of scripture" which, defined by the "Chicago Statement on Biblical Inerrancy," includes a statement that "Scripture is without error or fault in all its teaching."[5] However, the commandment to keep the Sabbath holy by ceasing from labor *seems* to contradict Jesus' preference for mercy. So how can all of Scripture be "without error or fault" if the commandments and Jesus say opposite things?

The solution to this apparent contradiction is in the purpose of God's law, rather than in the simple words of the law. As Jesus demonstrates in the Sermon on the Mount, I can abide by the simple words of "Do not commit adultery" and yet be filled with lust because the law has penetrated my actions but missed my heart. And, to the point of this passage, I can cease from all labors on the Sabbath and yet work so hard at keeping the law that I find no rest in God. In Mark 2:27, we see this clearly in Jesus' teaching that "The Sabbath was made for man, not man for the Sabbath." In all things, even our time management, God is for us and our good.

What we learn from Matthew 12:6-8 is that: a) Jesus is greater than the temple, b) mercy took precedence over law, and c) that the Law is derived from Him. In comparing Himself to the temple, the dwelling place of God, Jesus reveals Himself to be the Creator God incarnate, the One who worked to hang the heavens and root the earth and who rested from all His labors. The One who called our existence into being is the One who bids us to find rest from our strivings in Him. By emphasizing mercy above sacrifice, Jesus reveals the ignorance of the Pharisees, not only to His deity but to the law which they tirelessly work to keep. Finally, by claiming that the Son of Man is Lord of the Sabbath, Jesus emphasizes that as the Creator God incarnate, His heart is the heart behind the Law.

We are reminded we need to cease from the same futile attempts at earning our own worth in our drive for success. We can find rest in the One who has given our existence meaning and worth and who has affirmed that worth in His sacrifice given for our lives. God has called us to new life, life lived in Christ, with rhythms of rest and work, play and study. If we can begin to see ourselves as worthy of God's love and attention for His sake and not our success, then we can also rest from our insecurities that lead us to ignore the inherent worthiness and dignity of our neighbors.

But how do we effectively communicate this message to a generation of women who define themselves by their productivity?

Scripture shows us someone in Matthew 12 whose value in society was low *because* of his inability to produce. Jesus once again is confronted by the Pharisees on the Sabbath when He enters the synagogue. Noticing a man with a shriveled hand, they plot to "bring charges against Jesus," baiting Him to heal the man on the Sabbath. Therefore, they ask, "Is it lawful to heal on the Sabbath?" (v. 10). Jesus responds by pointing out both their hypocrisy and their lack of love: "Which one of you who has a sheep, if it falls into a pit on the Sabbath, will not take hold of it and lift it out? Of how much more value is a man than a sheep! So it is lawful to do good on the Sabbath" (vv. 11-12). The value of this man was not in his ability to be a productive member of society; he was crippled and in need of the support and resources of his community. Jesus loves him and says, "'Stretch out your hand.' And the man stretched it out, and it was restored, healthy like the other" (v. 13).

When we disciple young women and tell them to embrace and *accept* their weaknesses rather than hide behind a busy schedule, we may not help them pursue worldly success, but we will help them on their journey of sanctification toward deeper dependence and rest in Christ. How? We do this by allowing ourselves and our weaknesses to be seen by the women we disciple. We need to acknowledge that we ourselves can find a false satisfaction in busyness and pursuing what we think makes us appear to be "the best" employee, or mother, or the woman who is the most fit with the healthiest diet. They will witness God at work in our lives as we depend on Christ and they will see Him tend to us like the man in the temple in Matthew 12. As we are honest about our weaknesses and our need for dependence on Christ, the next generation of women that we disciple in our churches will witness older women who are secure in God's love for them, rather than insecure and in need of the affirmation based on accomplishments. When we practice Sabbath rest and encourage the women to whom we minister to rest and worship God, we are pointing them to pursue Jesus rather than success. Christ is the only one who gives us all ultimate rest from our striving when we acknowledge our need for a savior to redeem us from the sin of finding rest in our accomplishments. For today's Gen Z women, we need to communicate to them what may seem like a radical truth—that true rest and joy come only in knowing God.

Catherine Cook has an MDiv from Gordon-Conwell Theological Seminary. She serves as Director of Outreach and Discipleship with Reformed University Ministries (RUF) at her alma mater Harvard University.

DISCUSSION QUESTIONS

1. If the law is given for man, not man for the law, what does that tell us about the way we should view ourselves? What about how we should view our neighbors?

2. If you are older than Gen Z, do you struggle to identify with the new generation? Do you think you can relate to their idols of success and their identity being caught up in their production?

3. In what ways have you struggled to see yourself as worthy of love outside of your own efforts? How can you share your struggles in open but appropriate ways with those you are discipling?

4. How can you gently encourage young Christian women to value God's love above their own productivity? How can you encourage them to look to their neighbor and their neighbors' needs?

1   According to the research group Barna, members of Gen Z, who were young during the Great Recession of 2008, have come to equate financial stability with happiness. *Gen Z: The Culture, Beliefs and Motivations Shaping the Next Generation* (Ventura,CA: Barna Group, 2018), 12-13.

2   Neusner, Jacob. *A Rabbi Talks with Jesus* (Montreal: McGill-Queen's University Press, 2000), 3-4.

3   Ibid, 5.

4   Ibid, 2.

5   "Chicago Statement on Biblical Inerrancy." eSource. http://www.danielakin.com/wp-content/uploads/old/Resource_545/Book%202,%20Sec%2023.pdf

Chapter 17

Under the Hood: Driving
the Engine Towards Racial Healing
Lisa Robinson Spencer

Recently, I visited the Appomattox Court House site close to Lynchburg, VA. This landmark site is where General Robert E. Lee of the Confederate Army surrendered to Union General Ulysses S. Grant after Union troops had defeated Confederate troops. The museum presents the varying perspectives of this apex of the Civil War that drew this conflict to a close. But underneath the veneer of peace lies the disposition that prompted the conflict in the first place, one that did not die with the conflict but would continue to raise its ugly head for many decades to follow. The disposition is simply this: people of African descent were not entitled to the same rights and privileges as white citizens. The factors behind the Civil War were varied and intertwined, but its heart was to uphold or abolish the right to maintain chattel slavery.

Much has changed since the conclusion of the Civil War. Laws that were enacted to bar African-Americans from fully participating in American citizenry no longer exist. Though decades would be marked with persistent biases and opportunities to thrive were stymied by deeply entrenched racial bias in the broader culture, much progress would be made noted with the celebration of many "firsts" of accomplishments by African-Americans. I think it's safe to say that many biases have eroded though that hasn't fully taken away the presence of racism. Since the Fall in Genesis 3, evil inclinations of mankind have manifested in various ways and produce prejudicial thinking, hate, and ill will towards others. This is precisely what the concept of race has infused. We need to consider the trajectory of progress and the recognition that all men and women truly are created equal.

We cannot be lulled into thinking the church has been innocent with respect to race relations. The American evangelical church, and particularly denominations such as Southern Baptists and Presbyterians, were not exempt from this way of thinking and, furthermore, were complicit in upholding cultural norms that denied persons of African descent equal footing in society.[1] Regardless of the progress that has been made, the record does not lie. In fact, some conservative evangelical churches were some of the fiercest defenders of slavery and Jim Crow. Non-white Christians were actively barred from worship and deemed unworthy to share the same space. The same evangelical leaders who loudly proclaimed the gospel of Jesus Christ actively opposed the Civil Rights movement.[2]

Given this lengthy historical track record, discussions involving racial reconciliation in the church have been pursued for good reason. History has served as a good reminder that not all men and women were considered worthy of equal value and dignity. Regardless of how much progress has been made, such an extended legacy of infractions presses in the minds and bears on the souls of many people of color. At the heart of the cries of lament lies this one question: Is the same mentality that accepted chattel slavery in America, enforced Jim Crow laws, and treated non-white brothers and sisters in Christ as inferior still present in the church even if in subtle ways? How has this even subtle mentality impacted our ministry to women and how we relate to women in our churches who are different ethnicities or from different socio-economic backgrounds?

Any opportunity to recognize where a whole classification of people are devalued, disregarded, and dehumanized, particularly where that has occurred within the church, ought to result in sober reflection on where a failure to love others has occurred. As Christians, we have a mandate to consider others as more important than ourselves (Phil. 2:3). This means taking into account all dynamics in play of one's experiences. What are the personal histories that have impacted us? What are our fears? How have we been shaped by our experiences, perhaps even a familial legacy of racial injustice?

Problems start to arise when the lens of our perspectives are so divergent. On one side of the spectrum, regardless of how much progress has been made, there is a consistent lament by people of color who feel that every instance of contemporary transgression is a fresh reminder of the history's ugly noose. Every publicized event that has even the faintest tinge of racial injustice will open deeply felt wounds that entrenched biases are still a part of the fabric of our society. This lens sees a perpetuation of racism.

On the flip side, a different perspective emerges, one that cannot readily relate to the anger and sadness, particularly whenever publicized instances occur. Those looking through this lens cannot easily relate to lament, and so a discomfort occurs and grows with every mention of race and particularly any subtle or not so subtle charge that white people still might harbor prejudicial attitudes in their hearts. At times there can be blanket accusations of racism as if all white people are guilty. This certainly can raise the hackles, particularly where one does not believe herself to have attitudes of racism. This lens will want to maintain the status quo and desire for all such conversations to cease.

I often get the impression that we are responding more to the language that gets tossed around to describe racial infractions. When phrases and terms like white supremacy, systemic racism, white privilege, and oppression are used, especially considering the legacy of racial disparities that have existed in this country, it can garner either affirming or hostile reactions depending on the perspective of the hearer.

I fully understand that these terms are not meaningless. Where infractions exist, we must tend to them. We can't just simply oppose the use of words because we are uncomfortable and unwilling to see beyond a limited perspective. We must also strive to be judicious in our examination of where our brothers and sisters actually stand with respect to race and experience in the church. Are we making sweeping allegations without the benefit of the doubt? Are we really hearing what our sisters of color are saying about their experiences?

I have observed that the more we press into this topic, something other than reconciliation has taken place. Because such disparate perspectives exist, the conflict of vision causes fractures, suspicion and even downright hostility. Camps form with an "us vs. them" mentality. The ones with a sensitized observation to even the slightest hint of racial disparities will readily bring charges that oppression still exists, and racism still needs to be addressed. They will readily acknowledge and vocalize not only the historical legacy but also the present realities. To varying degrees, this camp will express dissatisfaction with the present state of race relations and insist that issues need to be addressed further. On the flip side, those who just want it to stop will also stop listening and may even lob accusations of division towards those who bring such charges.

Because camps have formed around the issue of race relations, this causes tension that impedes the process of reconciliation. We busy ourselves with trying to prove how the "other side" is not adhering to Christian ethics. Or worse, we disregard applying the gospel to this issue. We question motives. We assume a lack of caring, that "their" position undermines the work of the church. The epistle of James issues a sober caution in this regard, "What causes quarrels and what causes fights among you? Is it not this, that your passions are at war within you?" (James 4:1). At the heart of the war within us quite possibly lies selfish ambitions, the desire to uphold one's dignity. How can we ever heal with such a war in our midst? How do we get past the animosity that arises between the camps? I contend that as long as we respond according to our visceral reactions and don't get to the root of the trouble, we will never get to the place of healing.

One of the biggest issues I see with respect to racial healing is using the concept of race as the means to bring healing. In reality, race was constructed to create a hierarchal system whereby one class was deemed superior and one inferior. This hierarchal system emerged out of Europe based on economic trade that soon evolved into a full-blown denial of personhood towards those of non-European descent.[3] Scripture was used to denote the sub-humanity of those who were deemed biologically deficient and justified by dominant power structures.

It is in this vein that racial superiority reared its ugly head. Hatred based on biological factors, i.e., melanin, infested a whole group of people based on a notion that God never approved. It was a false concept derived from human imaginations. It is a construct derived as an outcome of the Fall.

If we are going to be serious about healing, I think we have to move beyond race. We have to reconcile how and why there is still a problem with respect to prejudicial attitudes, biases, and lack of concern for the other. That goes as much for women who unwittingly uphold racial superiority as well as the ones who fight to overcome it. We must examine the dispositions in our own hearts about imposing the sins of the past onto present day circumstances. We must also examine if we are ignoring legitimate concerns. It does us no good to continue the fight over the use of terminology or to lob accusations as if all whites are guilty at all times. In order to address sociological disparities within the church, we need to anchor corrections in descriptions that Scripture provides. I think this is an important factor to consider related to racial healing.

CHECKING IN SCRIPTURE TO CHECK OUR HEART

So, I suggest that we dig deeper to get at the real trouble. This is what I mean by getting under the hood. When a car is not driving right, the components that make the car run must be diagnosed. We can't simply keep saying the car is not running right and fight over whether it is or not. No, we need to diagnose the engine.

At the core of racism lie dispositions that can readily be seen in Scripture, dispositions where superiority/inferiority dominate. Right after the Fall, in Genesis 4:1-11, the story of Cain and Abel readily demonstrates this impetus to malign and elevate oneself over the other. The desire to dominate over another rose up accompanied by hate, pride, jealousy, anger and pompous justification. And it moved on from there as God's people grew more numerous and His divine revelation towards His creation became more detailed; the impact of the Fall infested families, tribes, and nations displayed throughout the Old Testament narrative.

By the time Jesus' earthly ministry came to fruition,

Gentiles were considered outsiders and unworthy to receive the same promises of God's good intentions. Samaritans were deemed inferior because of their hybrid nature as a result of being scattered after Assyria defeated the Northern Kingdom in 722 BC. Even though Jesus' revelation of Himself was to the Jew first (Matt. 10:5-6), His ministry involved acceptance of Samaritans and Gentiles as holding equal value in the kingdom of God based on their belief in Him.[4]

Yet, superior/inferior dynamics persisted after Jesus' resurrection. In Acts 6:1-4, the Grecian widows were being overlooked at the Lord's Table. It's no stretch of the imagination to consider why this was so. Jerusalem had been the hub of early Christianity based on its significance in the Old Testament, and Hellenistic Christians were being marginalized. How was this rectified? The church recognized that a certain population was being overlooked based on a disposition that deemed them inferior. While the issue was their Gentileness, the deeper problem rested in an attitude of superiority that resulted in infractions.

While not related to ethnicity, James 2:1-3 illustrates how disparities in group dynamics work out from similar attitudes. The poor experienced marginalization from the dominant group (the rich). James gets to the heart of the matter in speaking to partiality to follow the royal law of love, "You shall love your neighbor as yourself" (2:8).

Jesus told His disciples as He is telling His present-day disciples, "They will know you are my disciples by the love you have one towards another" (John 13:35). Jesus demonstrated what this love looks like: a willingness to lay down your life for the sake of the other. A lack of love lies at the core of hostile and dismissive attitudes towards one another. Throughout periods of overt discrimination in American history in the church, this lack of love resulted in sins of partiality, the active denial to consider others as equally valuable as image bearers of God. This is why we need to move beyond race if we are ever going to heal. In the case of the Greek widows in Acts 6 and the poor in James 2, the solution was to consider the other as an equal heir of the kingdom of God.

Scripture speaks to infractions that occur between groups that are rooted in specific dispositions. Where there is failure to consider the other as equally valuable, corrections rest in affirming equality according to how the other is treated and deemed important, not an anthropological identity. The church cannot afford to allow the overarching culture to define these infractions according to the false construct of race. This leaves us in a recycled loop of animosity that's sourced in finding equal value in race itself. Racial superiority existed for so long because "whiteness" was the norm by which all else was set. The corrections cannot come by upholding "blackness" or "brownness." Solutions must be rooted in how God defines the problem. From that vantage point, I'm increasingly gravitating towards the concept of partiality as described in James 2 because that is precisely what has transpired, and it is in line with the language of Scripture. Christians must disentangle from the cultural captivity of race and think differently about how we are supposed to relate to one another.

The image of God can only be fully realized in the reconciliation that Christ wrought. Ephesians 2-3 dismantles this notion of "racial" hostilities that has been ingrained in American culture for so long and compels us to relate to one another according to our identity in Christ, first and foremost. But this relation also compels us to examine where such partiality has existed in our hearts and continues to exist. We must consider how cultural norms—yes, even within the church and in our women's ministry—have been defined. It is only through this reality that any real reconciliation can occur, where we can deal honestly with real differences of cultures and experiences. It is here that the image of God corporately manifests to the world, the counter-cultural paradigm of Christ's kingdom.

Lisa Robinson Spencer has a Master of Theology (ThM) degree from Dallas Theological Seminary and blogs at www. theothoughts.com. She has also previously contributed to Reformed African-American Network (now named *The Witness*).

DISCUSSION QUESTIONS

1. In what ways do you see the sin of partiality still playing out in the church and in women's ministry? What are cultural norms that could marginalize others?

2. In what ways can women in your church foster Philippians 2:3 in action, to consider the other as more important than ourselves? Does your women's ministry encourage women in your church to really take time to hear each other out without wanting to make corrections?

3. We all can have prejudicial biases towards those who are not like us and draw conclusions of others based on stereotypes. In what ways can we regularly examine our hearts to consider our own biases towards those who are not like us?

---

1   For an in-depth discussion, see Joel McDurmon, *The Problem of Slavery in Christian America: An Ethical-Judicial History of American Slavery and Racism* (American Vision Press, 2017), 223-383. In this part II, McDurmon presents factual evidence of southern churches' actions towards support of slavery. Also see In *Defense of Virginia* by Robert Lewis Dabney that portrays the prevailing disposition in consideration of support.

2   See *For A Continuing Church: The Roots of the Presbyterian Church in America* (P&R Publishing, 2015) for a detailed treatise of opposition to integration and dismantling of Jim Crow laws.

3   Anjana Cruz, "Europeans invented the concept of race as we know it" https://timeline.com/europeans-invented-the-concept-of-race-as-we-know-it-58f896fae625; John Cheng, "Africans, Slavery, and Race" https://www.pbs.org/race/000_About/002_04-background-02-03.htm; Boris Barth, "Racism" http://ieg-ego.eu/en/threads/europe-and-the-world/racism.

4   For example, Jesus' interaction with the Samaritan woman at the well in John 4:1-38 shows His revelation of Himself towards her so she may believe. Also, see Jesus' interaction with the Canaanite woman in Matthew 15:21-28 demonstrates His acceptance of her based on her faith in Him.

Chapter 18

A Word to the Leadership Wives
Catherine Chang

Wives of the officers or pastors of a church are in a unique situation with respect to the life of the church. Our relationship to the rest of the body can often be complicated and riddled with expectations. It can also be a wonderful reminder of how the Lord works in His body. As the wife of a leader, you experience a great deal. You get hurt or disappointed. You are sometimes tired—physically, spiritually, and emotionally. If this is you, you are not alone in your challenges! There is hope and comfort. There is also a call to press on.

OUR GREATEST CALLING
First, a reminder—our highest calling in life is not to be the ruling or teaching elder's wife. In Scripture, we see descriptions of the qualifications of officers, but no such description of the elder's wife. The reason is because there is no such office. You probably think, "Of course there is no office of elder's wife!" but in practice, I believe that many leaders' wives live as though there were. We place on ourselves (or have thrust upon us by other church members) the belief that because we are married to an officer of the church, we, too, are called into "special" service.

We most certainly do have a high calling on our lives—we are called to a life in Christ, and it is *this* call that defines us. Perhaps we have gotten so wrapped up in trying to meet the expectations of church members (or defy them completely), that we find ourselves continually trying to either garner others' approval or pretend we couldn't care less. How do we re-orient ourselves? The answer may be simple, but I believe the good news must become good again. The awe of being called into a relationship with our sovereign God at the cost of His own Son should impact us profoundly each time we reflect on it, but for so many of us, the wonderful news of the gospel has become rote. What does it look like to cherish the good news as a teaching or ruling elder's wife? How do we live out the glorious calling we have, first and foremost as a daughter of the King?

LIVING OUT OUR CALLING

Love God first. "And he answered, 'You shall love the Lord your God with all your heart and with all your soul and with all your strength and with all your mind, and your neighbor as yourself'" (Luke 10:27). You must also love His Word. Remember how you loved Him before the daily-ness of life consumed you. How many of our challenges would look different if our perspective were funneled through the lens of a heart that truly seeks God? All the petty thoughts, complaints, fears of the judgment of others, a sense of not measuring up, the urge to compete—they are insignificant when we set our eyes on the marvelous light of the Savior.

Love your family. One of the most powerful ministries God gives to us as elders' wives is to raise up our children in the Lord and to support our husbands. What does this look like? If we look to Scripture as our guide, one helpful passage is Philippians 2:1-11. In it we see that the love of Christ is supremely humble, and Paul calls all believers to have this same love. To love our families in this way means to love as Christ loves, for His sake. It is a call not to love in a way that is ultimately self-serving, self-glorifying, or self-satisfying (though even this kind of love can possibly look good on the outside), but to love in a way that brings glory to our God and draws our families closer to Him.

Does this call to love and support our husbands look different for us whose husbands are officers of the church? If we examine the text of 1 Timothy 3, we see that elders are to be above reproach, self-controlled, hospitable, able to teach, and good managers of their households, just to name a few. In order for our husbands to be the men of God they ought to be, we must be the support they need. Naturally, this partnership will look different in each couple, but at the very least, we must strive to love our husbands well. They are only human, and they have been given a noble and often difficult task. They will not always lead perfectly in the church or in our homes. They will fail and struggle, but we must be reminded that our marriage covenant before God was to love them through it all.

Loving our husbands well is not easy and, at times, feels impossible. I know there are times when your husband is not loving you as he should, is not giving you the time you desire, has not followed through on his promises to you, but during those times, do you turn inward and withdraw? lash out in anger? distract yourself with your children or work? Or will you turn, broken and empty-handed to our Lord, the only One who can truly satisfy the longings of our hearts and love us perfectly? It is only in finding our hope in Him that we can in turn love and help the one He has given us, even when it seems impossible to do so on our own.

Love the church. Probably one of the most difficult things about being married to an elder or pastor is how much time you spend at church. Meetings, Bible studies, counseling sessions, events, crisis situations—these are all vying for your husband's attention along with his regular job (if he is a ruling elder) and family. It would be easy for us to resent church members and the church for requiring the time of our husbands so frequently. What do we do if we are frustrated? We remember. Remember that God called us out of death into life in a messy community filled with sinners like us (Eph. 2:5, 4:4-6, 5:8). Remember when we are weak and that weakness brings us to our knees, it is there we find His strength to sustain us (2 Cor. 12:10; Matt. 11:28). Remember that God, in His wisdom, has called our husbands to love this body. Remember that we, too, are called to love it (Eph. 4:16).

THE REALITY

As I talk with pastors' and elders' wives, common themes run through my conversations. While we may know intellectually that we can live confidently and freely in Christ, without a burden of people's expectations, reality is not that simple. Here are some of the issues I experience as a pastor's wife, and I hope these will encourage you to know you are not alone.

We know things. As elders, our husbands are privy to all the information in the church. As their wives, some of us are the recipients of much (at times too much) of what is weighing on them. Some of us are able to handle this information with wisdom and grace. Others of us are prone to judging, pride, or gossip. Wherever you may find yourself, I encourage you to do a heart check in this area. If you haven't already had the conversation with your husband, this is a great time to open up a discussion about your communication with regard to church matters. How much do you need to know? How much should you know?

We carry a special burden. Being the wife of an elder does bring a particular weight. Some of the most encouraging elders' wives I know have talked with me about how hard it has been, not because of the many hours their husbands put in or the expectations of people, but because they see from a unique perspective how much the church is hurting and in need of the leadership and care of the pastor and elders. The combination of seeing hurts and having access to information means that we need even more wisdom and grace to learn how to build up the body rather than tear it down. We must watch our own hearts and pray for wisdom and understanding to take what we know and use it to point people to Christ. One particular aspect we must be mindful of is that our thoughts and opinions have a great impact on our husbands—even more than we realize. When we are quick to respond with criticism or anger against someone or complain about decisions that are made, we impact our husbands and their leadership. Am I saying that we have to be guarded even with our spouses because they are leaders? No. I am saying that if we frequently respond harshly with anger or criticism, we need to stop and examine our own hearts, for our own good and for the good of the church.

We are often stretched thin. Some of the most amazing women I have met are wives of leaders. Each person is gifted for service in the body, and leaders' wives are called on to use their own gifts in the church. Often, church members have expectations that we are required to serve differently simply because we are married to leaders. We can have those same expectations of ourselves, or we can be controlled by the expectations of others and find ourselves overcommitting for the wrong reasons. Yes, wives of leaders are gifted, and yes, Scripture calls all of us to use our gifts for God's glory. However, if we are caught up in this pattern of doing, it is easy to keep doing and lose sight of our reason and purpose for serving. We serve because we have been loved by God and bought with a price (Gal. 1:10; 1 Cor. 6:20). We have been given a new identity (2 Cor. 5:17), and so we walk in accordance with who we are (Eph. 4:1).

We are resigned or refrained. There are some of us who have made the conscious decision to take a step back from serving in any capacity. Perhaps you were hurt by people in the church or burned-out from past service and want to distance yourself. Maybe you are put off by people's expectations and consciously live in defiance of them, perhaps even justifying this action in the name of freedom in Christ. If this is you, I would challenge you to spend time honestly considering where you are in relationship to the church. Are you hurt or bitter? angry or resentful? Are there specific people with whom you need to seek reconciliation? Are there past situations that define you more than your identity in Christ? If the answer to any of these questions is yes, I pray you would begin restoring the brokenness you uncover. We are all broken in different ways, but we love a Savior who specializes in making broken things whole again (John 4:29).

A WORD OF ENCOURAGEMENT

First, you are known fully. The God who formed you and predestined you to adoption into His family knows everything about you (Eph. 1:5; Ps. 139:13). He knows all your doubts, insecurities, and secret failings. He sees you when you are lonely, frustrated, and overwhelmed. He is with you in your struggles, disappointments, and despair. Through it all, He rejoices over you and calls you His precious child. You are known fully, and you are loved completely by God.

Because of Christ's love, a love that knows even the darkest parts and still chooses to love, you can love graciously. You will know things about people that they will want to hide, but you have the opportunity and privilege to love them in the darkest parts of their lives, and this will visibly show them the grace of Jesus.

As you grow in genuine Christ-like and sacrificial love for the church, you can serve joyfully. It is easy for us to get mired down in the routine of doing, serving, and giving week after week, but as we keep our eyes on Christ, as we are reminded of the incredible goodness of the gospel. As we grow in our love for God and His people, we can press on and be poured out, not just as an elder's or pastor's wife, but as a redeemed daughter of the King.

Catherine Chang received her MDiv in biblical counseling from Westminster Seminary in Philadelphia. She and her family reside in Southern California where she serves as the children's ministry director at her church.

DISCUSSION QUESTIONS:

1. What are difficulties you face as an elder's or pastor's wife? How do you typically respond to these difficulties?

2. In which areas of life does the good news of the gospel need to become good again to you as a leader's wife?

3. Which of the common themes (in "The Reality" section of this essay) resonate with you? Explain.

4. What encouragement would you give to other elders' wives?

5. How are elders' and pastors' wives in your church connected to one another for encouragement?

6. If you are in women's ministries leadership, how can you practically come alongside your pastors' and elders' wives to encourage them?

Chapter 19

BODY WORKS:
Mobilizing Women for Service
Donna Dobbs

I f you serve in your church, you will eventually hear the
cliché, "Twenty percent of the people do eighty percent
of the work." Sometimes this statement is made because
volunteers are nearing burn-out, or perhaps it's frustration
from members of a leadership team wondering why, once
again, no one has signed up to serve. Sometimes women are
afraid to step up to serve because they are intimidated by
seasoned, mature women who have taught women's Bible
studies for more than a decade. In women's ministry the most
important thing you can do to help women in your church
mature in service and in faith is not one-to-one discipleship
or personal counsel. It is engaging them in service to God
through the local church.

We see it here in the book of Ephesians, God's handbook
for the church. Here God gives practical instructions for the
church, and here we find God explaining how His church
grows, not numerically, but spiritually.

*But grace was given to each one of us according to the measure
of Christ's gift. Therefore it says, "When he ascended on high
he led a host of captives, and he gave gifts to men." ... And he
gave the apostles, the prophets, the evangelists, the shepherds
and teachers, to equip the saints for the work of ministry, for
building up the body of Christ, until we all attain to the unity
of the faith and of the knowledge of the Son of God, to mature
manhood, to the measure of the stature of the fullness of Christ*
(Eph. 4:7-8, 11-13).

Verses 7-8 say our gifts are derived from Christ's authority (kings led a parade after victories in war), and the gifts we now possess (booty from the battle) are won through Christ's victory over sin and death (Satan). These gifts, given to us, are expressions of Christ's authority and generosity and are the means of defeating sin and growing in grace. We are to use them to build up (disciple) the Body of Christ (Eph. 4:12b), because they are intended to help fulfil Christ's purposes for the church (Eph. 4:12-13), which include that leaders equip others for the work of ministry in the Body. By equipping others, the Body is built up so that it will be "mature, attaining to the whole measure of the fullness of Christ."

What are the results when people are prepared for service? Maturity. Verses 12-13 tell us, "so that the Body of Christ may be built up until we all reach unity in the faith and in the knowledge of the Son of God and become mature, attaining to the whole measure of the fullness of Christ." Christ actually gives Himself to the church through the collective gifts He gives, and people exercising those gifts are essential to increasing spiritual maturity in the church because Christ works through them.

If equipping the saints is essential for the church to become mature, how is it accomplished? How are people identified and equipped to give their time and talents to the church for service over a lifetime? Here are some practical aspects of identifying and training members for ministry.

CALLING PEOPLE TO SERVE

The process of selecting leaders is not best done when the need is urgent and immediate. It takes time for people to think through how serving in a ministry could fit into their lives, so when recruiting, suggest serving in a particular capacity well in advance of the need.

Remove as many obstacles to service as you can. One reason recruiting can be difficult is that too many responsibilities lie on too few people. It can be challenging to recruit leaders because you are asking them to do more than they are able to do. A Bible study requires teaching, but it also requires administration, preparation and study, and communication. Teaching alone requires an average of eight hours of preparation weekly. Additionally, the class requires some administrative details: someone to choose the study, order books, collect money, set a calendar, find a meeting place, make refreshments, publicize the study, and communicate with the students. It's a heavy load, and those tasks do not require teaching gifts. The reality is you can't recruit enough leaders because you don't have enough leaders; therefore, build a team to share responsibilities. Some who do not want to teach will gladly organize the study. Some who do not want to be in charge will gladly keep the records and communicate with students. Once support is built in, shared responsibility makes the load lighter, and people are more likely to commit to serve and will serve over a longer period.

In an age of busyness and mobility, it is a supernatural response for people to agree to sacrifice their time, efforts, and plans to serve others for Christ's sake, so prayer and trust in God are essential to finding the right people for each responsibility. That may sound too obvious, but fear and frustration will prevail if trust in God's guidance and provision is not the foundation of your work.

Over decades of ministry I have recruited thousands of people to serve in the church, and I have a secret to share: I have a love/hate relationship with recruiting. It is hard work that occurs sometimes under a lot of pressure. Good theology and a rightly placed self-identity are essential to persevere at times. But you are not asking women to serve for yourself, you are asking for them to serve in God's Kingdom. It is not a personal favor; it is service to God.

One of the benefits of recruiting people for service is that it provides an opportunity, and the privilege, to enter into other people's lives. When people are asked to serve, they will share their lives with you and let you know about their illnesses, relocations, aging parents, rebellious children, or job difficulties. You may never have known those things, so even a "no" response opens the door for ministry to people whom you believe are potential ministry leaders. God's "no's" are as good as His "yeses."

RECOGNIZING LEADERS

People are naturally drawn to others who may have big personalities and the ability to engage others with their eloquence or style, but don't confuse style with substance. Every true Christian leader leads with character and commitment.

Look for qualities such as these:

A worshipper. After all, your goal is to lead more people to worship God, so of course, being a faithful worshipper (public and private) is essential (2 Cor. 2:14-15).

A student of the Bible. Do they love the Word? The Word of God is our wisdom and our compass. Some leaders make decisions based on what they want, think, or feel. Christian leaders must be students of the Word so that Scripture (and not the wisdom of the world) guides them (1 Cor. 1:25; 2:12-13).

A growing Christian. Do you see spiritual growth in this person? Do they hunger and thirst for righteousness? Do they avail themselves of opportunities to learn more about and serve Christ? Do they put their own lives under the authority of the Word of God (2 Cor. 5:14-15)?

How they exhibit authority. Do they humble themselves for the advantage of others, or do they advantage themselves to the disadvantage of others? Are they willing to sacrifice for others, not living as they please by letting personal comfort and convenience determine their decisions (2 Cor. 1:6-7, 12)?

How they communicate. Leadership includes being able to think critically and articulate goals, processes, and rationales. Can they put their thoughts and plans into words in an orderly manner that is easy to understand and follow? Can they break the big picture down into component parts so that people can see and do what needs to be accomplished (1 Cor. 1:4-7)?

A heart for a particular kind of ministry. A person who has administrative gifts and would be good at coordinating the women's retreat might not have teaching gifts. Be a student of the women in your church and take note of what captures their hearts. Once they are engaged in particular ministries, they will likely become long-term, productive servants in those areas (Phil. 4:1).

PREPARING PEOPLE TO LEAD

There is not one superior method that trumps all others in discipling people, but there are a number of methods that complement each other, both one-on-one and in groups.

IN ONE-ON-ONE TRAINING:

Meet to talk about the purposes of the group. Many groups have disintegrated because people either didn't know or didn't support the purpose of a group. For instance, a Bible study group is not primarily a prayer group nor a support group. Is there prayer and support in a Bible study? Of course, but if you are not careful to guard the main purpose, it can get lost. Haven't you seen this happen?

Have you ever been in a Bible study where you couldn't get through the study questions because sharing prayer requests went too long? You feel very unspiritual saying, "No, don't pray," but the truth is that the explanation of the requests takes most of the time. Every decision ought to be filtered through the question, "How does this support the purpose of this group?"

Talk with them about the people and personality of the group. There are lots of resources that train leaders how to guide discussions without being side-tracked by personalities. There are talkative people and there are quiet people. There are opinionated people and there are needy people. A leader needs to know how to bring the quiet person out, how to set parameters around the talker, how to soften the opinions of some, and how to lift those who are discouraged. Many small group Bible study books cover those skills.

Provide suggestions for commentaries, websites, and other materials that can be resources for them. Encourage personal study. Most people don't think they know enough about Scripture to teach it; therefore, encourage them to do a daily chronological reading of the Bible for their devotions, or you might suggest good, readable books on Bible overviews or theology. Scripture builds on scripture, and teaching and studying just one book of the Bible connects you to many other passages and topics elsewhere in the Bible. Their knowledge of Scripture grows exponentially as all of those things interconnect.

Shepherd them. Regularly communicate with your team of leaders to see how things are going, encourage them if things get tough, and support them in personal areas of their lives such as marriage, parenting, death, and illness. Show you value each of them as a person by walking beside them in life. These are expressions of caring found in Christ-centered communities (1 Cor. 9:19; 2 Cor. 12:15a).

Connect them with a mentor. Often it is possible for an older, more experienced leader to meet with a potential leader. That mentor can explain what she studies, what resources she uses, and how she prepares. She explains what is important in that ministry (1 Tim. 1:3-7).

In group training. The insights of others can open doors of understanding unavailable to us when studying alone. Build in some time for leaders to connect with others for their personal growth. A few ideas might include:

- Provide something they value, such as having a pastor or another seasoned teacher train all of your leaders.
- Take the summer to do a study together with all teachers/ leaders of any age.
- Recommend one of the recent biblical or theological overviews or studies, or encourage them to take a seminary course online.

If multiple groups study the same topic at different times, meet together regularly to review their lessons. This provides opportunity for rich discussion with other leaders who have a mutual passion for the Word.

SUPPORTING LEADERSHIP

Build in support for them. Recruit someone to substitute for them if something unexpected comes up or to give them a break a couple of times during the study.

Create community among your leaders. Have regular leadership meetings with all your leaders for prayer, updates, input, and long-range planning. Keep them in the loop about plans for the future. Have your pastor come and pray for them. Connect them with others in leadership so that they begin to think of themselves not as solo leaders, but as part of a whole community of leaders.

Equipping women for kingdom service and watching God bless our natural efforts with supernatural results yields eternal benefits that far outlast you and the leaders in your church. It is the way God grows His people and His church.

Donna Dobbs has a master's degree in Christian Education from Reformed Theological Seminary. She is the Women and Children's Director at First Presbyterian Church (PCA) in Jackson, MS.

DISCUSSION QUESTIONS

1. By virtue of His authority, Christ gives gifts to the church to help it mature. How does that impact your view of recruiting and training leaders?

2. Many people are reticent to recruit people to serve in ministry. Instead, they do everything themselves. What are the disadvantages of this approach?

3. Have you ever considered that using your gifts is one way that Christ shares Himself with the church? What eternal

effects have you seen displayed by virtue of the service
of saints?

4. Think through what kind of training would work in your
   setting. What kind of individual study would be possible for
   your teachers? What kind of one-on-one study could you
   employ? Is there a way for your teachers to study together
   in groups?

Chapter 20

All the Single Ladies in the Church
MyChelle Pinkerton

C hristians are called to live holy lives and glorify God by loving Him and loving people (James 1:27). We are to live joy-filled lives as a testament to God's goodness and grace in saving us from our sins (Titus 3:4-8) as we seek to serve those around us. While engaging others both in our churches and in our communities through acts of service and hospitality in a world consumed with pursuing pleasure, we are called to make Christ known—to be salt and light in this world. Therefore, the flavor of our lives should be distinct and appealing as we reflect the light of Jesus.

One only needs to watch the local news or scroll through her social media feed to see that the world is a dark, broken place. People are lovers of themselves and seekers of pleasure. Therefore, followers of Jesus must be intentional about participating in the life of a healthy, biblical church. It is in the community of faith that believers find encouragement to walk faithfully with Christ, while also knowing they have the added benefit of relationships with fellow Christians who care about them and point them to biblical truth. God never intended for believers to live a life of faith in isolation (Heb. 10:24-25). Our brothers and sisters in Christ help us stand firm in a culture that celebrates and promotes sin. Fellow believers cover us in prayer, point us to the gospel, mourn when we mourn, and joyfully celebrate with us (Rom. 12:15). They help us with discernment and are used by God as instruments of correction for our blind spots (Col. 3:16) and struggles with sin.

TRANSFORMATION IN GOD'S HOUSEHOLD

As believers, our feelings and desires need to be examined before the Lord to ensure they align with His will for our lives. Our natural bent is to desire ease, comfort, and pleasure. Oftentimes, the work God has for us will not be easy or pleasurable, but it will be for our good and His glory (Rom. 8:28-30). We need to be open to what God is doing in our lives, so we can work with Him as opposed to working against Him (1 Peter 1:6-9)—and this is done best in community.

As Christian women, we connect with our church for accountability and spiritual growth and allow God to use our relationships to expose the motivations of our hearts. It is in the context of close Christian friendships that we learn just how selfish or unforgiving we can be. It is where God teaches us how to handle conflict in a biblical manner, express emotions in godly ways, and ask for help in areas of struggle or need. When sinful hearts are exposed, the truth of God's Word shines a spotlight on the use of manipulative and sinful behaviors we use to get our needs met (1 John 1:7).

Godly relationships provide a safe environment for vulnerability so that we can grow more into His image. This kind of transforming work often takes place in a godly marriage. So, what are Christian single women to do? How do they go about engaging in the life of their church and establishing accountability? How do they balance their dreams of one day growing in grace with a marriage partner (or in biblical friendships if called to singleness) while remaining in God's will to live holy lives—lives that glorify God and serve others well (Eph. 2:10)?

SINGLE WOMEN IN THE LIFE OF THE CHURCH

In order to disciple single Christian women, it is critical that the church and especially women's ministry be mindful to view its events and outreaches through the eyes of a single person, realizing that singles, too, need channels for transformation and service. Single women are not just concerned about "waiting well for their spouse to arrive"; they are also concerned about how to grow in their faith, serve God, be good stewards over their finances, and make sound career decisions. Their hearts' desire is to bring honor and glory to God while deepening their walk with Him. Leaders of the women's ministries should review their events to ensure they are well-balanced and just as relevant for single women as they are for married women.

Likewise, singles have the responsibility of actively engaging in the community in which the Lord has placed them. Singles need to look for ministry opportunities in the church that appeal to their unique spiritual gift mix. Their spiritual gifts are given to them by God to be used to benefit the church body (1 Cor. 12). Church leaders as well as women's ministry leaders should proactively and intentionally ask singles to participate in all sorts of ministries in the church, not just obvious ones. Ask singles to lead Bible studies (if they are spiritually mature women), to be on church committees (many working women have lots of professional experience and skills they can offer as they serve on a church committee), to mentor teenage girls, or to visit the elderly. Often church leaders unwittingly exclude singles from serving the entire church body.

The church uses small groups, Bible studies, Sunday school classes, and Sunday worship to promote community and transformation. However, as a single person, it is not always easy to plug into a community group. In some churches, singles, across age groups and life seasons, are grouped together in one Bible study or Sunday school class. A recent college graduate has very different needs from a recent divorcee or a woman in her 40s who is well into her career. Oftentimes, small groups are solely made up of families or married couples. The single woman may feel like the "odd person out" and lose motivation to attend a small group regularly. How can church leaders intentionally provide a welcoming environment for singles to get involved in these opportunities for community?

Women's ministry and church leaders need to offer events and Bible studies on evenings and Saturdays and make events accessible to working women, including single working women. When planning small group teaching seminars and Bible studies, church leaders need to avoid always having content that is overtly focused on marriage or parenting. The majority of Scripture does not focus on particular seasons of life, but rather its truth applies to all (women or men, single or married). Offer Bible studies with content that does not exclude single women so that a church's small group ministry is a welcoming environment for singles.

The single woman who is growing in Christ in the context of Christian community will benefit from intentional considerations by fellow church members. For example, one way married couples and families can encourage single women is by grafting them into their lives—by making them an honorary member of their family and inviting them over for meals and including them in family activities. Everyone has a desire to belong and be included.

TITUS 2 ACCOUNTABILITY

In addition, single women need safe places to learn how to identify and communicate their feelings and learn biblical ways to navigate conflict. Therefore, it is also beneficial for singles to seek out mentors, women to "do life" with and learn from (Titus 2), who are spiritually mature women open to walking alongside other women through life and who possess the attributes of godliness single women want in their own lives. Leaders of women's ministry need to provide ministries that encourage women to develop relationships with "spiritual mothers."[1] With some training, potential mentors can not only help younger women navigate through their spiritual and emotional health, but also help hold them accountable in areas of sin struggles and temptations. Accountability is a key ingredient for a successful mentoring relationship.

Accountability is defined as an obligation or willingness to accept responsibility or to account for one's actions.[2] In other words, accountability is giving someone permission to get into your life and give you biblical rebukes when necessary. For single women desiring to live holy lives, accountability is essential. As a single woman, it is too easy to live a fragmented life. Church life usually does not intersect with work life, and social life may not intersect with church life. A fragmented life makes it easy for singles to hide themselves. In some circles, singles may be very active and appear to be well-known, but the truth is no one may really know them. They might share just enough to appear engaged but hold back from sharing their real struggles, hurts, or fears. For women desiring to live a godly life, this is dangerous. It is easy to rationalize away sinful behavior or compromise when a single woman only answers to herself. It is harder to fight off the lies Satan attempts to plant in the mind—lies like believing that marriage and child-bearing are the "best" ways to honor God and to have a fulfilled life, as well as lies meant to accuse and destroy.

An accountability partner can ask the hard questions—questions designed to expose the motivations of the heart. A mentor will be able to see and call attention to patterns of sinful behavior that result in unintended consequences. A mentor's intention is not to discourage but to point to Christ so that the Christian grows more and more into His image. Exposing her true self to this level of accountability is risky for a single woman because it requires vulnerability. She also needs discernment and guidance in choosing a mentor because not every woman is mature enough to handle this level of vulnerability. This is where a women's ministry can come alongside single women in the church. Women's ministry can identify, train, and deploy godly, theologically sound, seasoned women to be resources to women in the church to disciple women (including single women).

Sometimes a single person's desires turn into demands to God in regard to wanting to be married. The heart's motivation (Matt. 6:33) towards singleness needs to be evaluated. How does the single woman who desires to be married prevent resentment and bitterness from taking root in her heart if God intends for her to remain single? How does she overcome her anger, disappointment, and bitterness about her singleness? She needs to be actively involved in a doctrinally sound, healthy church. A healthy church is made up of emotionally healthy and spiritually mature people.[3] We become emotionally healthy by examining our heart motivations, processing what surfaces, and healing from past hurts in the context of the truth of Scripture. One option to help women examine their heart motivations is to see a professional counselor. A counselor is a good resource for helping to unpack past experiences which have shaped us and to answer questions such as: As a single woman, do you know what expectations you have of people in relationship with you, and are you confident in your ability to communicate those expectations effectively? How do you view yourself and how do you view God in relation to yourself?

When I was single, the Lord blessed me with a wonderful spiritual mother. She was witty and feisty and a fierce lover of Jesus. She was intentional about getting to know the real me. By my late twenties, I was adept at presenting a version of myself that the people around me would find pleasing. I desired to remain in God's will and live a holy life; however, I kept my heart "safely" locked away. I was busy serving God in youth ministry, but at the same time I was bitter and angry with God for my being single. Satan used my bitterness, and I would hide behind a mask and put distance between myself and God as well as distance between myself and others.

During a particularly low point, I remember reaching out to my mentor, and sharing that I had made some poor decisions and was having a difficult time. I expected her to end our friendship due to my sinful behavior, but she did the exact opposite. She pursued me fiercely. My mentor is small in stature, but she is a mighty warrior of God. She pointed me to truths in God's Word and prayed for me. She provided me with biblical counsel and cried with me. My heart had been shattered, and the Lord used her to lovingly heal those hurts. As I look back at that time in my life, I am forever grateful I took the risk of opening my life to my mentor and being accountable to her. Since then as I have experienced many more valleys, and even some mountaintops, this godly woman has been there every step of the way. God has used her in my life, and she has blessed me in ways I cannot put into words. Because of her example, my desire is also to disciple other young women.

To those who are single, God's call to abundant living isn't just for those who are married. Marriage does not lead to a perfect, trouble-free life. The apostle Paul makes it clear that married life is often a more difficult road to travel than single life (Eph. 5:22-23; Col. 3:18-19). In marriage, couples can struggle to keep a balance between seeking to please God and seeking to please one another (1 Cor. 7). A season of singleness should not be viewed as punishment or as a heavy burden. Strive to live out your God-given calling in spiritually mature ways. Use the gifts He has blessed you with to serve the body of Christ well. Seek out accountability as a means of guarding against Satan's tactics to discourage and defeat you. Be confident in knowing the very good work our Lord began in you will be brought to completion—He will do it! (Phil. 1:6).

MyChelle Richardson-Pinkerton is a licensed marriage and family therapist who enjoys working with couples as they seek to live abundantly in their marriage relationship.

DISCUSSION QUESTIONS

1. As a single woman, how are you engaging in your church body? What activities do you wish you could do that you are not currently doing?

2. Who makes up your accountability network? If you do not have a network, what prevents you from establishing an accountability network? Do you have an older, spiritually mature woman in your life? What does she do to specifically point you to Christ?

3. Women's ministry leaders, how are you intentionally engaging and including single women in your ministry Bible studies, church committees, outreaches, and events?

---

1   Hunt, Susan. *Titus 2 Tools: Building a Titus 2 Ministry* (Lawrenceville, GA: PCA Committee on Discipleship Ministries, 2016).
2   www.merriam-webster.com/dictionary/accountability
3   Pete Scazzero, *Emotionally Healthy Spirituality* (Nashville: Thomas Nelson, 2006), 17-19.

Chapter 21

Who Will Care for the Caregiver?
Elizabeth Reynolds Turnage

C lad only in a gray t-shirt and adult diaper, my dad slouched in his wheelchair. He moaned again, mumbling indistinct words, then poked his skeletal arms into the air, motioning for me to lift him. What had happened to the distinguished dad I had known all my life—the sharply dressed English professor who enunciated every syllable, the witty lecturer who could turn a phrase like Shakespeare himself? Aging had happened. Late-stage prostate cancer had happened. Dying had happened.

Sickness, dying, and death are not always grueling for the caregiver, but quite often, they are. Just ask the approximately 37 million female family caregivers, many of whom are faced with the agony of Alzheimer's, the afflictions of cancer, and the anguish of end-of-life decisions. While many female caregivers serve only temporarily, caring for a spouse or parent recovering from knee replacement surgery or a bout with atrial fibrillation, others serve day-in and day-out for years and years, caring for aging parents, disabled loved ones, or family members with addictions or mental health issues. It is no wonder that family caregivers show signs of chronic stress.

According to the National Alliance for Caregiving and AARP study of 2015, "approximately 43.5 million caregivers have provided unpaid care to an adult or child in the last 12 months."[1] The Institute on Aging study of 2016 revealed, "Upwards of 75 percent of all caregivers are female, and may spend as much as 50 percent more time providing care than males."[2] Christians will not be surprised that women serve as caregivers far more often than men. It could be argued that our exquisite design as life-givers uniquely equips us to be caregivers.[3]

As the number of female caregivers occupying (or absent from) church pews on Sunday mornings increases, women's ministry and church leaders must ask the crucial question, "Who will care for the caregiver? And how?" First, we must equip ourselves with a robust theology of suffering and death.

A BIBLICAL THEOLOGY OF SUFFERING AND DEATH

Suffering and death originated with the fall. In the beginning, God designed His image-bearers to live forever, reigning and ruling over His cosmos. Then, Satan slithered onto the scene. The first man and first woman slipped down the tripping path of the seducer, grabbing the forbidden fruit, eating their way to death. Our forebearers' first sin, their active rebellion against the Sovereign God, cost them, and us, dearly—decay, division, disease, death, and other d-devastations entered the world. As D.A. Carson explains, "Evil is the prime cause of suffering, rebellion is the root of pain, sin is the source of death."[4]

While we recognize that suffering and death originated with the fall, we must not assume that all suffering and death are the direct result of individual sin. Jesus corrects this mistaken assumption when His disciples ask Him about the cause of a man's blindness (John 9). They assume that either the blind man or his parents sinned. Jesus tells them, "'It was not that this man sinned, or his parents, but that the works of God might be displayed in him'" (John 9:2-3).

Caregivers sometimes suffer from the erroneous belief that their loved one's illness is caused by sin or by inadequate faith. We can assuage this suffering by reminding caregivers that God does not always explain why people suffer and die (Job), and that sometimes, God answers "no" to our prayers for relief (e.g., Paul's thorn in the flesh, 2 Cor. 12:7-10).

God is sovereign over suffering and death. Just as no sparrow falls to the ground apart from the Father's will, the only suffering that can bruise us is that which God allows (Matt. 10:29-31). As the *Heidelberg Catechism* puts it, "He also preserves me in such a way that without the will of my Heavenly Father not a hair can fall from my head; indeed, all things must work together for my salvation."[5]

Caregivers will at times feel crushed as they witness their loved one's bodily distress. In such times, we can gently remind them that they can trust in the God who rules and reigns over all things for our good and His glory (Rom. 8:28).

God transforms suffering and death. God transforms suffering and death for His good purposes: to make us more like Christ, to display His glory, and to advance His kingdom. Understanding God's purposes in suffering can bring hope to the caregiver.

While our union in Christ dictates that we will suffer (Luke 9:23; Phil. 3:10), our union in Christ also empowers us to endure suffering in a way that makes us more like Christ.[6] Suffering moves us from self-reliance to God-reliance (2 Cor. 1:9). As God comforts us in our afflictions, we will in turn comfort others in their afflictions (2 Cor. 1:3-4). We even learn to rejoice in our suffering, "knowing that suffering produces endurance, and endurance produces character, and character produces hope" (Rom. 5:3-4).

Suffering and death also serve to display God's glory, allows the gospel to be preached, and His kingdom to advance. After cataloguing his multiple afflictions, Paul concludes, "For it is all for your sake, so that as grace extends to more and more people it may increase thanksgiving, to the glory of God" (2 Cor. 4:15). As Pastor Tim Keller explains, "When believers handle suffering rightly, they are not merely glorifying God to God. They are showing the world something of the greatness of God—and perhaps nothing else can reveal Him to people in quite the same way."[7]

God responds with compassion to those who lament suffering and death. As we will see in the next section, the caregiver often needs encouragement to grieve her losses. Scripture provides a vast vocabulary for lament, "a prayer in pain that leads to trust."[8] Over one-third of the Psalms are laments, and entire books of the Bible, including Job and Lamentations, feature powerful expressions of grief. How does God respond to lament? To Job, to David, to others who lament, God does not offer explanations; instead He offers reminders of His extravagant mercy and might (e.g., Ps. 22:22-31; Job 38-41).

For one who lamented, though, God responds not with explanation but with execution. In the Garden of Gethsemane, Jesus borrows words from David's lament, "My God, my God, why have you forsaken me?" (Matt. 27:46; Ps. 22:1). While God responds to David's lament with reminders of His goodness, He remains silent when Jesus cries out. Jesus, unlike any other lamenter, must be truly forsaken by God. Jesus must, "for the joy set before him, [endure] the cross, despising the shame . . ." (Heb. 12:2). What joy was set before Jesus? The full confidence that in His separation from God, He purchased our reunion with God. The full confidence that His death and resurrection would defeat suffering and death.

Because of the resurrection, we have hope in suffering and death. As caregivers are jolted by the healthcare rollercoaster, they desperately need hope, something believers have in abundance. While we may groan today as we eagerly await our full adoption and our redeemed bodies (Rom. 8:23), we keep scanning the horizon for our Lord, who is surely coming back one day soon (Rev. 22:7). In that day, God "will wipe away every tear from their eyes, and death shall be no more, neither shall there be mourning, nor crying, nor pain anymore, for the former things have passed away" (Rev. 21:4). Pastor Eric Tonjes, whose wife is dying of cancer, describes the hope of the resurrection: "Without the resurrection, this brief grasping and wilting we call life is nothing. With the resurrection, it is the heartbeat of infinite life."[9]

Armed with a sound theology of suffering and death, we can come alongside the caregiver, believing that suffering and death will ultimately give way to glory for the Christian.

CARING FOR THE CAREGIVER

As the caregiving population continues to increase, women's ministry and church leaders must learn to bear the burden of the female caregiver. Consider the following ways to address the caregiver's need.

Identify the caregivers in your congregation. It is natural to focus on the suffering of the sick, but in so doing, we sometimes miss the caregiver's misery. Consider Jesus, who not only looked for suffering people but acted with compassion when He found them (Luke 7:11-17; Matt. 9:36; John 11). Though we can't raise anyone from the dead as Jesus did, we can offer life by noticing and caring for the caregiver. To identify caregivers, take note of who is absent from church activities and consult the list of sick people in the church, considering who cares for them.

Pray for caregivers when you pray for the sick. Pray for the caregiver, and whenever possible, pray *with* her. Visit or call, and ask permission to pray. Your praying voice can soothe her frenzied spirit. Text, email, or write a card, and send a written prayer. When our 22-year-old son had to undergo four brain surgeries in a seven-month period, I sometimes struggled to form the words to pray. Written prayers sent by friends gave me the vocabulary and voice to praise, petition, and thank the Lord.

Recognize the emotional, psychological and spiritual cost of caregiving and address these costs with a rich theology of suffering. According to an *American Journal of Nursing* study, "Caregiving has all the features of a chronic stress experience. . . ."[10] These features include "physical and psychological strain," "high levels of unpredictability and uncontrollability," "secondary stress in . . . work and family relationships," and "high levels of vigilance."[11] Ministry leaders are particularly well-equipped to address guilt, spiritual struggle, and grief, three contributors to caregiver stress.

Many caregivers are weighed down by guilt: intense feelings of failure and inadequacy. We can address this burden with gospel-grounded hope, reminding the caregiver frequently that only Christ is sufficient to be another's Savior. We can invite the caregiver to confess both her failures and her sins to the One who sympathizes with her weaknesses (Heb. 4:15). We can further remind her that God's grace is sufficient in her weakness, that indeed, His strength is made perfect in her weakness (2 Cor. 12:9).

As the caregiver witnesses her loved one's agony, she may at times struggle spiritually and grieve deeply. The ministry leader can enter this grief and encourage the caregiver to cry out to the

God who hears. When my father was agonizing through his final days at the same time our son was recovering from brain surgery, I often felt acute distress. Wise and loving friends listened to my lament, "How long, oh Lord, will this sorrow last?" They wept with me (Rom. 12:15), gently pointing me to the comfort Scripture offers: we groan with the entire creation as we eagerly await our future hope, certain redemption (Rom. 8:22-23).

As ministry leaders, we will also need to address another aspect of grief pertinent in an increasingly post-Christian society. Many caregivers will be anticipating the death of a loved one who does not profess Christ as Savior. Author Nancy Guthrie offers three crucial reminders for this particular heartache: first, only God can evaluate another person's heart (Luke 23:42-43); second, we can trust God to judge fairly (Gen. 18:25); and third, God is far richer in mercy than we are (Eph. 2:4).[12] These three biblical truths offer powerful hope to those grieving in uncertainty.

If we avoid quick-fix answers to profound questions about the loved one's suffering, instead pointing to the reality of gospel hope, we can relieve some of the stress caregivers experience.

Educate and encourage caregivers regarding the urgency of self-care. Kelly Markham, LCSW, ACHP-SW, explains a potentially lethal cycle that can develop for the caregiver. The caregiver believes that she alone can tend to the loved one properly; the loved one often reinforces that belief. Under the chronic stress of caregiving, the caregiver's health suffers. Committed to caring for her loved one, she neglects her own healthcare. Such neglect of self-care has been shown to lead to an earlier and higher mortality rate for caregivers as compared to non-caregivers.[13]

The ministry leader can emphasize the critical need for self-care, encouraging the caregiver to attend to her own physical, emotional, and spiritual needs. Church care teams can provide respite care, freeing the caregiver to make medical appointments, attend Bible study, run errands, or exercise. Where skilled care is required, the church might assist in paying for a trained worker.

Educate and equip church leaders and members with essential knowledge and wise counsel regarding end-of-life decisions. In the twenty-first century, a broader array of life-sustaining and life-prolonging measures is available than ever before. While these measures can benefit the patient, they can also cause harm. Dr. Kathryn Butler, former critical care surgeon, explains the confusion for caregivers around end-of-life measures. Patients often lack clear advance directives; doctors, patients, and caregivers resist discussing death; and complex medical vocabulary is incomprehensible to laypeople. Because of the complexity and confusion, caregivers often feel intense anguish over end-of-life decisions.

Such anguish can be avoided if Christians, who know that death has lost its sting (1 Cor. 15:55), will prepare to die well. As Dr. Bill Davis explains, Christians are empowered to enter such discussions wisely because we have Scripture to guide us, we know the value of human life, and we have the hope of eternal life. Ministry leaders can help caregivers by arranging opportunities for completing advance directives and by offering curricula such as that written to accompany Davis's book.

Assist with practical needs. Church ministries or individuals can organize meals so that the caregiver is not overwhelmed with a glut of food. Youth groups can be deployed for yard work or car washing. Individuals can offer to run specific errands. A Bible study group can gather to clean the house. Consider the everyday life of the caregiver and imagine what tasks need to be done, then offer to do one of them.

Ministry leaders can also help by recognizing the financial struggles caregivers often face. Paying bills, filing for insurance, and making plans for long-term care are among the myriad chores which add to the caregiver's heavy burden. Church leaders or members who have professional financial expertise might come alongside the caregiver to help with tasks or to offer guidance. Alternatively, the church may temporarily subsidize professional financial counsel. In addition, the church may offer financial assistance for a season when a health crisis causes shortfalls.

In all of these ways and more, ministry leaders can help to lighten the caregiver's burden of suffering.

THE WEIGHT OF GLORY

Tucked under his covers, final fleeting breath drawn, my dad seemed at last to be at peace. I stood over him, remembering my two-year journey of caring for him. He had suffered, yes—the at-first slow demise of cancer, then the finishing blows of bone pain. I had suffered, yes—grief at his demise, and, in the end, my utter inability to shield him from the crush of cancer.

But suffering and death were not given the last lines—glory, joy, and hope stole the scene. I had enjoyed the profound privilege of being a life-giver in my father's dying days. I had experienced the extraordinary lightness of being carried by Christ's body, the church. To know such care is to know the weight of glory that makes our suffering short, our troubles light.

Who will care for the caregiver? I pray it will be me. I pray it will be you. I pray it will be our churches.

Elizabeth Reynolds Turnage, MEd and MACS, writer, teacher, and story coach, is the author of *The Waiting Room: 60 Meditations for Finding Peace & Hope in a Health Crisis.*

DISCUSSION QUESTIONS

1. Review the "Biblical Theology of Suffering and Death" section. What gospel realities will help you care well for the caregivers in your church?

2. Have you served as a caregiver? If so, what have been the challenges, what has brought you comfort, and what do you think ministry leaders need to know to minister to caregivers? If not, find a caregiver and ask her about her challenges and comforts.

3. Review the "Caring for Caregivers" section. Choose one or two ways to serve a caregiver in your congregation.

4. Does your church have leaders or curriculum in place to assist

members with preparing advance directives and/or learning about end-of-life issues? If not, what steps might you take to create these opportunities?

5. Using what you know about the caregiver's suffering, handwrite a note with a prayer for one of the caregivers in your congregation and mail it to her. Include scriptural reassurance you think the caregiver needs to remember.

1   "Caregiver Statistics: Demographics," Family Caregiver Alliance, National Center on Caregiving, 2016, https://www.caregiver.org/caregiver-statistics-demographics.
2   Ibid.
3   See Karen Hodge's introduction to this book for more on women as life-givers.
4   D.A. Carson, How Long, O Lord?: Reflections on Suffering and Evil (Nottingham: Inter-Varsity, 2006), 40.
5   "The Heidelberg Catechism, Question 1," The Heidelberg Catechism, http://www.heidelberg-cate-chism.com/en/ (accessed June 12, 2019).
6   For more on suffering and our union in Christ, see Rankin Wilbourne, *Union with Christ: The Way to Know and Enjoy God* (Colorado Springs: David C. Cook, 2018), Kindle Edition, Loc. 3083.
7   Timothy Keller, *Walking with God through Pain and Suffering* (New York: Penguin Books, 2016), 175.
8   For more on God's purposes in suffering, see the excellent article by Scott Hafemann: "A Call to Pastoral Suffering: The Need for Recovering Paul's Model of Ministry in 2 Corinthians," Southern Equip, Summer, 2000, http://equip.sbts.edu/publications/journals/journal-of-theology/sjbt-42-sum-mer-2000/a-call-to-pastoral-suffering-the-need-for-recovering-pauls-model-of-ministry-in-2-corin-thians/ (accessed June 20, 2019).
9   Mark Vroegop, "Strong Churches Speak the Language of Lament," The Gospel Coalition, April 08, 2019, https://www.thegospelcoalition.org/article/strong-churches-lanuage-lament/ (accessed June 17, 2019).
10 Eric Tonjes, "Terminal Cancer, One Year In," EricTonjes.com (blog), March 20, 2019, http://www.erictonjes.com/2019/03/terminal-cancer-one-year-in.html (accessed June 17, 2019).
11 Richard Schulz and Paula R. Sherwood, "Physical and Mental Health Effects of Family Caregiv-ing," *American Journal of Nursing*, https://www.ncbi.nlm.nih.gov/pmc/articles/PMC2791523/ (accessed June 19, 2019).
12 Ibid.
13 Guthrie's full explanation of these principles is excellent. Nancy Guthrie, "Comfort When an Unbeliever Dies," The Gospel Coalition, May 30, 2017, https://www.thegospelcoalition.org/article/comfort-when-unbeliever-dies/ (accessed June 20, 2018).
14 I am indebted to Kelly Markham, Palliative Care Manager at Baptist Hospital Pensacola, for explaining crucial issues for caregivers, especially regarding dying patients.
15 Barbara M. Roberts, writing to ministry leaders, points out, "Our ability to help someone who is dying and the family of the dying person depends largely on our own attitudes regarding death." Barbara M. Roberts, *Helping Those Who Hurt* (Colorado Springs: Navpress, 2009), 62.
16 Kathryn Butler offers a comprehensive explanation of end-of-life measures in her book *Between Life and Death: A Gospel-Centered Guide to End-of-Life Medical Care* (Wheaton: Crossway, 2019), 29.
17 J.I. Packer offers an insightful explanation of why twenty-first century Christians do not prepare for death and dying as they did in past centuries. See J.I. Packer, *God's Plans for You* (Wheaton: Crossway, 2001), 201.
18 Bill Davis, *Departing in Peace: Biblical Decision-Making and the End-of-Life* (Phillipsburg, NJ: P & R Publishing, 2017), 38. This book has an accompanying curriculum.

Chapter 22

Fear, FoMO, and a Promise
Stefanie Formenti

As someone who works on a college campus, I regularly have interesting conversations with young women. If you were a fly on the wall in my office, you would hear something along these lines:

"I'm just *afraid* of making the wrong decision about my major."

"I know I should break up with him, but what if I never get married?!"

"Going with that internship seems so *scary*. What if I fail or disappoint people?"

"I'm just *fearful* of giving the wrong impression if I voice my opinion."

"What if I don't land a job I like, and I can't pay off my student loans?!"

Fear is a universally powerful emotion. It doesn't choose its victims according to race, gender, age, or economic status. It doesn't announce its impending arrival but strikes at unlikely moments in unbelievably poignant ways. Fear can paralyze, or it can spur to hasty action. It can skew reality, making it no little foe.

Even as followers of Christ, we struggle with fear on a daily (sometimes momentary) basis. Perhaps it is the fear of getting old, or losing our voice and influence, or having a failed marriage or rebellious kids. Maybe it is the fear of being alone, or being misunderstood, or being controlled. Maybe being vulnerable or generous or hopeful makes us want to run for cover.

It's not surprising that many of my conversations with college women deal with the issue of fear. These fears are real and, in a sense, can be boiled down to a common and growing fear among young people between the ages of 18 and 34—FoMO. This catchy acronym stands for the "Fear of Missing Out," defined as "the uneasy or sometimes all-consuming feeling that you're missing out—that your peers are in possession of more or something better than you." According to *TIME Magazine*, nearly three quarters of young people experience this phenomenon.[1] Directly correlated to the amount of time spent on social media sites like Facebook, Instagram, and Snapchat, FoMO is social anxiety characterized by the desire to stay continually connected to what others are doing. It's a "catch 22"—those who fear missing out on something better constantly check social media where they encounter firsthand all the things that they are *indeed* missing out on. Such fear often leads to anxiety, comparison, and excessive busyness.

ANXIETY, COMPARISON, AND BUSYNESS

With such constant connection comes a new kind of panic. Shelly Turkle writes, "People say that the loss of a cell phone can 'feel like death.' Whether or not our devices are in use, without them we feel disconnected, adrift."[2] In an effort to be in the know, we become attached to our devices at the cost of real relationship and community, living an anxious reality that can lead to pathological internet use. We are scared to unplug because we are worried that the world might leave us behind.

It's no wonder that this anxiety also lends itself to comparison and discontentment. Comparison is nothing new, but now, "keeping up with the Joneses" goes to new depths thanks to Pinterest. "Facebook, Twitter, Foursquare—they all broaden our scope for comparison. They also make it harder to feel good about your life's choices. Choice is an inherently stressful luxury, especially in a culture that suggests it's possible to have it all."[3]

When I lived in Brazil, I struggled with loneliness, and my smartphone became my lifeline. So, I spent an inordinate amount of time scrolling through images of my friends' lives on social media. What I thought would help me feel known to others actually led to a great struggle for contentment. I became increasingly frustrated that I couldn't go to Target or have Starbucks or celebrate the Fourth of July with fireworks and a cookout. Instead, I was stuck in a new place with a new language, food, and culture. Imagine my surprise when a friend confessed to me that she was envious of *my* "exciting" life as shown through my social media posts because she longed to travel and experience new places. At that moment I realized that the fear of missing out on the "American Dream" was contributing not to my good, but to an attitude of comparison and discontentment.

Moreover, FoMO can result in excessive busyness. In my current ministry context on a college campus, it's common to see students who are burnt out, overwhelmed, and crazy busy. They are afraid to create healthy boundaries lest they miss out on opportunities for fellowship, interesting conversations, or resumé-builders. Author Kevin DeYoung puts it this way, "We are busy because we try to do too many things. We do too many things because we say yes to too many people. We say yes to all these people because we want them to like us and we fear their disapproval . . . So much of our busyness comes down to meeting people's expectations."[4] When we step back and evaluate our calendars, we may be surprised at how many commitments we make out of fear—fear of disapproval, loneliness, or missing out.

Comparably, it is common for students to attend an event out of the fear that if they don't, they will miss out on something. Experiences are now valued when they can be shared with the hundreds of "friends" on social media rather than simply the present company. Watch what happens the next time you go to a concert or tourist destination. So much time is spent curating the perfect photo opportunity and so little time is spent actually enjoying the place or event itself. Even coffee with friends turns into a selfie opportunity. Why? Because we want to be seen as part of something, as a member of the "in" group.

THE GOSPEL SOLUTION

If we're honest, we can all see the ways that the fear of missing out has influenced our mindset and actions. FoMO, like other fears, is a force to be reckoned with. So, what can be done? With a quick Google search, you can have strategies for combatting FoMO at your fingertips. From taking sabbaticals from social media to practicing gratitude, researchers are keen to fix the unhappiness FoMO creates.[5] While these suggestions can be helpful, the fear of missing out is an issue of the heart and needs a gospel solution.

In Genesis, we read the creation account where a loving Creator breathes life into Adam and forms Eve from his side. He rejoices over them, calling this pinnacle of creation very good, giving them dominion and purpose. All the garden's blessings are theirs, and God walks and talks with them as a friend. In His goodness, God prohibits the couple from eating the fruit from one tree, because doing so would result in death. But, sin slithers in:

He [the serpent] said to the woman, "Did God actually say, 'You shall not eat of any tree in the garden'?" . . . But the serpent said to the woman, "You will not surely die. For God knows that when you eat of it, your eyes will be opened, and you will be like God, knowing good and evil."[6]

Satan approaches Eve and plants seeds of doubt. "Did God really say?" he asks. And then his words deepen her doubt by intimating that God is withholding something better from her. The serpent posits the idea that God doesn't want Eve to be like Him, that He wants to have the only true knowledge about life, that God's rules and boundaries are actually causing the first humans to miss out on something better. Essentially, Eve's doubt actualizes into sin because of FoMO. Eve fears that if she follows her Creator, she will miss out on something better.

They say hindsight is 20/20, but lest we judge Eve too

quickly, let's examine ourselves. Aren't we just like Eve? When we unearth and unpack our fears, whether it be fear of death, loss, sickness, or missing out on something, we discover the root of unbelief. We fail to remember and believe that God is who He says He is and that He will do all that He says He will do. We wonder if God's prescription for a whole life is that of a life missing out on something better. We doubt that His love for us is enough to give us abundant life.

According to Scripture, the cure for FoMO is not a list of strategies, but the necessary reorienting of our hearts to a posture of belief that God has never, is not currently, and will never withhold from us what is best. This is the power of the promise made in Genesis 3:15: "I will put enmity between you and the woman, and between your offspring and her offspring; he shall bruise your head, and you shall bruise his heel."

Here God is meeting Eve's FoMO head on. He is confronting her twisted theology of missing out on something better by promising to withhold nothing from her. Instead, He promises to send *everything*—His very own Son, Jesus, to bring redemption as far as the curse is found. The rest of the biblical narrative points to this promise, and then Paul exclaims in Romans 8:31-32: "What shall we say to these things? If God is for us, who can be against us? He who did not spare his own Son but gave him up for us all, how will he not also with him graciously give us all things?"

God has given us everything by giving us Jesus. Just as God did to Eve, He consistently and graciously confronts our fear of missing out by reminding us, through the Spirit, of His immense love for us. God loves us enough to give His own Son! Because of this, we can rest in the fact that He is withholding nothing from us! Instead of anxiety, we can have peace. Instead of comparing our lives to the lives of others, we can trust that this is the life God has allotted to us for our good and His glory. Instead of excessive busyness, we can create healthy boundaries, put down our phones, and rest.

THE GOODNESS OF GOD'S WORD

As I talk with college women, I find that although our life stages might be different, we actually struggle with the same fears. I, too, am often paralyzed with the fear of making the "wrong" decision or a fear of loneliness or of financial insecurity. Sometimes it seems like God is silent instead of present in our fears. We doubt God's goodness, faithfulness, and character as our good Father. We let doubt grow into sinful anxiety. We let fear dictate our schedules and relationships lest we miss out on something important.

This is why the study, application, and memorization of God's Word is so beautiful! When we immerse ourselves in Scripture, we "unplug" from the world's solutions for fear and, instead, reorient ourselves to the biblical narrative that we are citizens of heaven and heirs with Christ. When we marinate ourselves in the truth of Scripture, we remember and affirm that we have not been given a spirit of fear, but of power; we confess together that we belong to the One who owns all things and sustains all things with the power of His will. Because of Jesus and His work on the cross, we can cease our striving to be more, earn more, or do more. By resting in God's promises, we admit that the world spins without us, and we yield our hearts to the calming power of dependence on the God who has freely given us abundant life. We need not fear anything because we have a God who has come down to us as a man and given us His presence through the Holy Spirit. As a result, as daughters of the King, we know that we aren't missing out on anything.

Stephanie Formenti has an MA in Theological Studies (Covenant Theological Seminary). She is Chapel Associate for Discipleship at Covenant College.

DISCUSSION QUESTIONS
1. How does FoMO impact your daily decisions and routine?

2. Take a minute to list your fears. How is unbelief at the root of those fears? How does the gospel (the truth of God's abundant love in Jesus) confront your fears?

3. Often, our unbelief comes from our inability to remember.

List some passages of Scripture to commit to memory in your fight against fear. (Examples: Matt. 6:25-34; Ps. 27; Ps. 46:1-3; Isa. 41:10; Rom. 8:15)

4. In what ways do you see women in your church struggling with their fears?

5. How as a women's ministry can you address FoMO?

1 Eric Barker, "This is the Best Way to Overcome Fear of Missing Out," TIME.com. http://time.com/4358140/overcome-fomo/ (accessed April 14, 2018).
2 Sherry Turkle, *Alone Together* (New York: Basic Books, 2011), 16.
3 Hephzipah Anderson, "Never Heard of Fomo? You're So Missing Out," The Guardian.com. https://www.theguardian.com/commentisfree/2011/apr/17/hephzibah-anderson-fomo-new-acronym (accessed April 22, 2018).
4 Kevin DeYoung, *Crazy Busy: A (Mercifully) Short Book about a (Really) Big Problem* (Wheaton: Crossway, 2013), 35.
5 Linda and Charlie Bloom. "10 Ways to Overcome Fear of Missing Out," *Psychology Today*.com. https://www.psychologytoday.com/us/blog/stronger-the-broken-places/201501/10-ways-overcome-fear-missing-out (accessed April 28, 2018), or check out this movement at http://www.sabbathmanifesto.org/.
6 See Genesis 3:1-5.

Afterword

I have a friend who embraces spoilers and even reads the end of the book before reading the entire book. Perhaps you are scanning this book and turned here since you are wondering, in a nutshell, what is the point? Why women's ministry and why now? You may have heard the phrase, "There is no such thing as women's ministry only ministry." This is a short-sighted approach. Your church needs a women's ministry.

Specific ministry to women at this juncture of history is more relevant than ever. Even non-religious women want to connect to other women to be encouraged. In a *New York Times* article that highlighted a Los Angeles group that connects women over 50-years-old with other women to find friends, the author notes, "A study by the *Industrial Psychiatry Journal* published in *Psychology Today* showed a significant relationship between depression and loneliness in older people. It suggested that 'female friendships can be the key to happiness in older women, but they're not often treated as such.'"[1]

Our culture's pursuit of egalitarian relationships has diminished the significance of the relationship women have with each other as they create safe spaces to do life together. The deficit of gender specific friendships was seen in our culture as a missing component as the "#Metoo" movement unfolded and many women in crisis realized they have felt isolated and afraid to speak up about their crisis. They realized the importance of connecting to other women. Frankly, there must be room for women's ministry. A church without a women's ministry will not, for example, be able to effectively care for women in crisis. These women need other women, not men,walking alongside them.

But for Christian women, ministry to other women is more than just finding a BFF or being a Christian version of the Junior League. It is about helping women to know God through His Word, to be a committed disciple of Christ, to share the gospel with other women, to be involved in the life of their church, and above all else to worship and glorify the living God. Women's ministry does this by connecting women to the whole church, not by being a ministry in isolation.

This book is not designed to be comprehensive and to address all issues women face or to answer exegetically the specific role of women in the church when it comes to ordained leaders. It is meant to encourage church leaders to have a robust women's ministry based on a theological foundation from God's Word and not driven by personality or a few dynamic teachers or big annual events.

This volume is also not meant to be a how-to guide to give church leaders the 10 best steps to organizing a women's ministry, suggest specific Bible study materials, layout a discipleship plan for the women in your church, or provide a blueprint for how a women's ministry should be structured.

Rather, this book is an apologetic for a robust women's ministry at your church. Yes, your church should have a women's ministry. And your women's ministry needs to be contextualized for your community. Women's ministry events, leadership teams, and specific outreaches will look different in Los Angeles, Ohio, New York City, Alabama, Seattle, South Carolina, Nebraska, Connecticut or in the UK, South America, or Japan. But what women's ministries worldwide should have in common is a foundation built upon the Word of God.

Even if you do not have a formal women's ministry, women will connect and they will gather. Women are a vital part of any church's body life and ministry. Women have many gifts, experiences, and godly wisdom to impart to others, especially their sisters in Christ. May God use the women in your church for the expansion of His kingdom in the world.

Melanie Cogdill
Charlotte, North Carolina

1   Rozette Rago, "Finding Female Friends Over 50 Can Be Hard. These Women Figured It Out," *New York Times*, Dec. 31, 2018, https://www.nytimes.com/2018/12/31/style/self-care/finding-female-friends-over-50-meetup.html.

Acknowledgments

I love movies and see dozens of them every year. And I always sit through the credits, (sometimes alone in the theater) to see all the names of people who worked on the film. I try to read as many of the names as I can as they quickly scroll up on the screen. A film is much more than the director, screenwriter, actors, and executive producers. These credits are more than obligatory. I wish you could personally know each of these people listed—they are amazing people who make my life so much better, fuller, and richer because God placed these Christian brothers and sisters in my life.

Thank you seems like an insufficient phrase to express my gratitude to all those who have had a part in this volume. Thanks to the Presbyterian Church in America's (PCA) Committee on Discipleship Ministries (CDM), which equips and disciples the churches of the PCA and which published this book. I am especially grateful to Stephen Estock, the coordinator of CDM, for his godly counsel, advice, and theological insights as we discussed the content of this book. I am deeply thankful to Karen Hodge, PCA Women's Ministry Coordinator. Karen has been a friend for more than 18 years, but not only that, she has been a co-laborer with me in PCA Women's Ministry and is the epitome of a servant leader. Without Karen's godly leadership and encouragement, this book would not be a reality. She is a bridge builder and helped lead me to some of the new voices in this book I did not previously know before this project.

I truly appreciate Pastor Irwyn Ince who didn't even pause when I asked him to write the foreword but quickly agreed to write it. I am so grateful to him for his service and leadership in the PCA as our denomination considered issues surrounding women and ministry.

I am thankful that this book is a group project—it's the voices of many Christian women of different ages and races, but all with sharp intellects and insights. I am grateful to the contributors for their time, writing gifts, and patience even when I asked for multiple re-writes of sections of their chapters.

I am also indebted to the editorial skills and input of Marlys Roos, Teri Anderson, Abby Hummel, and CB Campano since no one pair of eyes is ever sufficient for written material. A very big shout-out to my Facebook friend, the writer Trillia Newbell who came up with the title for this book (which previously was quite ho hum and bland).

To my dear friend and sounding board Sarah Ivill, her input was vital, and her help with this project was invaluable. Sarah and I are members of the same church, and I'm thankful to Christ Covenant Church and specifically a few of the pastors on staff who gave input: Kevin DeYoung, Bernie Lawrence, and Brian Peterson (who lent me his commentary on Titus).

No project is worth pursuing without being thoroughly undergirded in prayer. Many thanks to the PCA National Women's Ministry team for their faithful prayers for this book. I consider it a blessing to be able to serve with them. I also want to thank co-workers who are faithful prayer warriors at the Christian Research Institute where I work as the managing editor. They have also given me flexibility in my job to be able to serve in PCA women's ministries.

This book is dedicated to Susan Hunt. More than 25 years ago, I met Susan when she stayed at my two-bedroom apartment in Escondido, California (located in the same courtyard as a sand volleyball court). As I drove her to and from a conference at my church, Susan patiently answered all my blunt questions about the roles of women in the church and women in ministry. After that it was Susan who encouraged me to become involved in regional and national women's ministry. And so, my journey in women's ministry began.

And to my husband, Dwayne, heartfelt thanks for his pro-bono work to layout and design this book. More than 20 years ago Dwayne encouraged me to be involved in women's ministries and still encourages me to pursue women's ministry opportunities. Words cannot fully express how thankful I am for his love and faithful prayers. I could not have embarked on or finished this project without his support. Dwayne and my two incredible sons Jack and Harry have made many sacrifices over the years for me to serve in women's ministry. It's a cliché to say your spouse is your better half, but anyone who knows us and meets Dwayne, knows it's completely true. He is the better half of our marriage, and I am thankful for the ways in which he points me to Christ.

Now this book is done, and I look forward to seeing how the Lord will use it to minister to women.

Melanie Cogdill
Charlotte, North Carolina

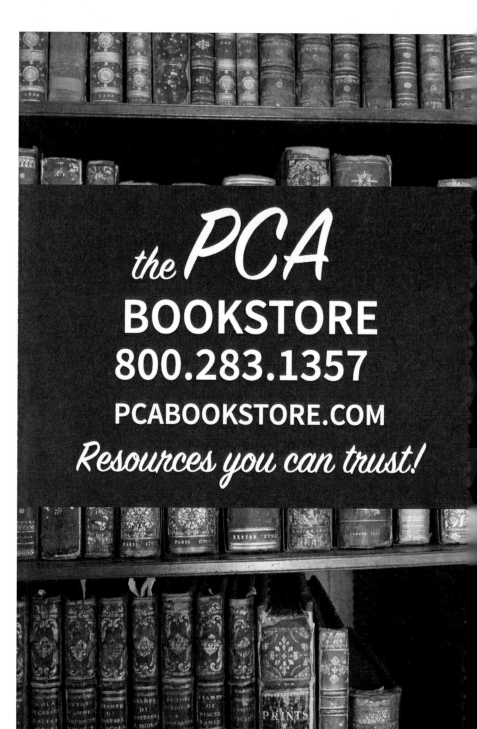

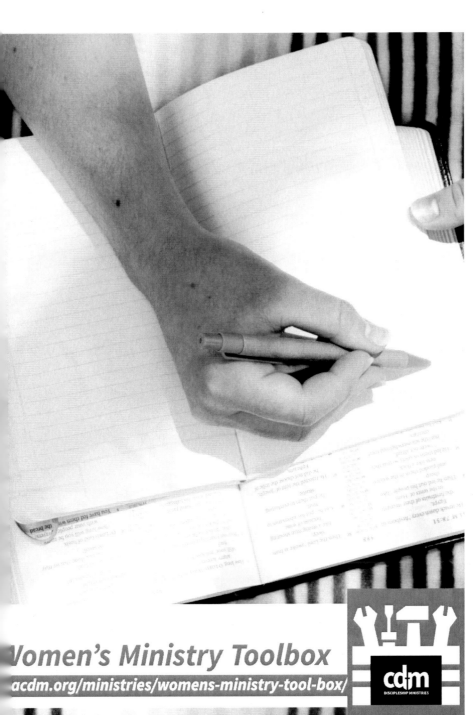

Women's Ministry Toolbox
acdm.org/ministries/womens-ministry-tool-box/

cdm
DISCIPLESHIP MINISTRIES